I Killed Pink Floyd's Pig

Inside Stories of Sex, Drugs and Rock & Roll

Foreword by Sammy Hagar

Beau Phillips

Seattle, Washington
Portland, Oregon
Denver, Colorado
Vancouver, B.C.
Scottsdale, Arizona
Minneapolis, Minnesota

ISBN: 978-1-59849-168-5
Library of Congress Control Number: 2014908215

Printed in the United States of America

Design: Soundview Design Studio

Peanut Butter Publishing
943 NE Boat Street
Seattle, Washington 98105
206-860-4900
www.peanutbutterpublishing.com

Table of Contents

Foreword

I grew up listening to rock radio. The louder the better.

I cut my teeth on bands like Led Zeppelin, the Stones and the Who. Hearing them on the radio inspired me to play guitar and sing. Man, there's no greater feeling than hearing your baby blasting out of car radio speakers, knowing that thousands of other people are listening.

Over the years, rock radio's been great to me. Along the way, I've visited lots of radio stations and made some great friends. Without radio's help, I would've been parking cars for a living.

Whenever I hit Seattle, I'd stop in to see Beau Phillips and the crazies at KISW. They gave me a shot and played my songs since day one. I'll never forget that.

Trust me, Beau has seen all of the wildness that went on backstage. And this book is loaded with amazing stories.

So, grab a margarita and let's rock!

Sammy Hagar

Preface

Once upon a time, rock gods ruled the earth.

The ground trembled as they swept from town to town, announcing their presence with thunderous chords. Legions of rock disciples flocked to their leaders. Ever devoted, they proudly wore shirts honoring their gods, emblazoned with a single name.

Zeppelin. Floyd. Clapton. Bruce. Ozzy. Slash.

This book celebrates the titans who shaped rock music for a generation, and beyond. It's a peek backstage during the decadent era of sex, drugs, and rock & roll. You'll get to know the bands that dominated the airwaves when rock was great. When air was clean. When gas was cheap. When Michael Jackson was black. When SNL was funny. When disco sucked.

A rock renaissance began to simmer in 1979, and it took fans on an exhilarating, seat-of-the-pants ride that lasted into the mid-90s. After years of marshmallow-soft hits and mind-numbing disco, rock stormed back with a vengeance. In a flash, the rock gods swung their hammers and wiped out disco with a single blow. They elbowed aside placeholder artists like Debbie Boone, Leo Sayer and Andy Gibb, ending their careers.

The rock gods punctuated the 1970s with a loud, hard exclamation point.

All of the planets aligned in 1980 as record labels, concert promoters, music stores and radio stations all feasted on a tasty smorgasbord of rock goodness. Wave after wave of iconic rock albums swarmed the FM dial and held the *Billboard* music charts in their brawny grip. Music fans reveled in an enchanted wonderland of Pink Floyd, Van Halen, Rush, Bob Seger, Tom Petty, the Who, ZZ Top, Ozzy Osbourne, the Stones, Queen, Ted Nugent, Bruce Springsteen, AC/DC…and the list goes on. For fifteen blissful years, those superstars were in their prime and released the finest albums of their careers. Meanwhile, new rock gods emerged, including U2, Guns' Roses, Bon Jovi, Def Leppard, Journey, Pat Benatar, Scorpions and the Police.

Rock fans gorged themselves. It was like standing in front of a musical fire hose, not wanting to miss a drop.

During this glorious era, rock ruled and every corner of the music industry thrived. What made this a uniquely special time was the spirit of cooperation. There was a perfect storm of exciting bands, prolific record labels, savvy concert promoters and destination record stores. But radio was the driving engine behind this rock revolution. Popular stations were the megaphone that evangelized to the masses and helped break artists on a national scale. Radio stations, labels, stores and promoters banded together to expose great, new music. This pay-it-forward collaboration had never existed before, and sadly will never happen again.

But it sure was fun while it lasted.

As the manager of influential rock stations and senior VP at MTV Networks, I witnessed the musical explosion from the inside. I was a fly on the wall when the almighty rock gods toured the land and built empires that have stood for decades.

This book will take you "behind the music" with funny, profound and outrageous stories. Over the years, I hung out with bands backstage, onstage and under the stage. Occasionally, I got invited into the inner sanctums of bands' dressing rooms, hotel suites, limos, tour buses and private planes. As you might imagine, I collected some amazing stories—and I borrowed some great tales from friends.

I had a bird's-eye view of rock & roll craziness that would make your head spin. If you're ready, I'll take you on a guided tour and introduce you to rock's biggest superstars. You'll take a red-eye flight with Keith Richards. You'll have beers with AC/DC, throw TVs with Led Zeppelin and party with Van Halen. You'll tear up hotel rooms with Joe Walsh and play golf with Jimi Hendrix's dad.

So strap in, and enjoy the adventure!

Acknowledgements

Beau Phillips would like to thank:

His sons - Julian Bogel, Rory Bogel and Ross Bogel. Laurie Cantillo, for her love and editing. Also David Cantillo, and Zach and Taylor Parsons.

Those who created the stories: Sammy Hagar, Robert Plant, Jimmy Page, Keith Richards, Mick Jagger, Pete Townshend, Pink Floyd, Van Halen, Eric Clapton, Tom Petty, Sting, David Lee Roth, AC/DC, Paul McCartney, ZZ Top, Joe Walsh, Smokey Wendell, Journey, Bryan Adams, the Fabulous Thunderbirds, Ann and Nancy Wilson, Sheryl Crow, Madonna, Loverboy, Foreigner, Joan Jett, Bob Geldof, Al and Jimi Hendrix, Pat Benatar, Bon Jovi, Jeff Beck, Sam Kinison, Lynyrd Skynyrd, Def Leppard, Bob Dylan, Dickey Betts, RATT, Ted Nugent, Jimmy Kimmel and Randy Bachman.

Story Contributors: Sal Cirrincione, Tim Sabean, John Lassman, Dave Hamilton, Tony Scott, Larry Sharp, Sky Daniels, Watts Wacker, Joe Wade Formicola, Joe Bevilacqua and Greg Gillispie.

His co-conspirators: Steve Slaton, Lee Abrams, John Bauer, Ken Kinnear, Mike Flicker, Gary Crow, Mike West, Bob Rivers, Cathy Faulkner, Scott Jameson, Robin Erickson, Steve West, Jim Carey, Andy Schuon, John Parikhal, Kirk Stirland, David Hazan, John and Cathy Langan, Joshua Simons, John Paul, Tim Maranville, Larry Harris, Dave Richards and the current gang at KISW, Bo Roberts, Stan Foreman, Larry Reymann, Judy Libow, Paul Rappaport, Mark Gorlick, Jim McKeon, Robert Nesbitt, Doug Cooper, Debi Lipetz, Jane Norris, Jeff Kragel, Ron Woodward, the late Lester Smith and Steve Young.

Photographer: Darrell Westmoreland Images…still the best.

Rock
THE
INK
FM 100
Rock
VAN HALEN
KISW
Rock
DEF LEPPARD
Rock
TOM PETTY
Rock
SAMMY HAGAR
KISW•FM 100
PAT BENATAR
KISW•FM 100
Rock
BILLY SQUIER
KISW•FM 100

Chapter 1

VAN HALEN's
STRIPPER INVASION

"An ounce of image is worth a pound of performance."
David Lee Roth

From the first time I set the needle down on Van Halen's debut album, I knew we'd struck gold. The band's raw power jumped out of the speakers. Their songs grabbed you by the ears and refused to let go.

Van Halen commanded your attention—no, they demanded it.

The rock radio jocks at KISW in Seattle wore out the grooves on "You Really Got Me" and jammed to the pelvic thrusts of "Runnin' with the Devil." Listener reaction to Van Halen came hard and fast as our request lines lit up. Rock fans couldn't get enough of the party boys from Pasadena.

From day one, my station got on board the Van Halen train, and we became fast friends with the band, their managers, their promoters and Warner Brothers records. Together, we transformed their new albums into events and their concerts into spectacles. Everyone knew that when Van Halen came to town, the party was on.

In 1981, Van Halen was firing on all cylinders, following a string of multi-platinum albums. Their concert tours sold out across the country, usually in a matter of minutes. Arenas were packed with devoted fans, decked out in Van Halen

T-shirts. Lead singer David Lee Roth emerged as the sexiest front man in rock, while guitar whiz Eddie Van Halen was hailed as "the new Hendrix." Van Halen was the first hair band, coiffed and glamorous in spandex, and tailor-made for MTV.

At one point Van Halen was selling so much concert merchandise that the band bought its own T-shirt factory. Then, they bought a rock station in Portland, Oregon.

That summer, I read that Van Halen was coming to our city. So, I called the band's manager, Noel Monk, and suggested, "KISW will be celebrating our 10th anniversary the same week that Van Halen is playing in Seattle. The guys will be here for two nights. Can David Lee Roth, Michael Anthony and the Van Halen brothers stop by our station before the concert?"

Monk considered it for a moment, then sighed, "Sorry Beau, I'd like to say yes. But their schedule is pretty tight. I just don't think they'll have time this trip."

Rock stars often came by for a visit before heading to the arena for their sound checks. But sometimes they didn't have time. I got that. But I was really disappointed the band couldn't find a few minutes for us. I couldn't help but wonder if Van Halen was just too big now. Maybe we were old news to them.

Fast-forward to the afternoon of Van Halen's first concert. It was about 2 p.m. on a hot June afternoon and anticipation for the show was running high. All day, the radio station's request lines had been flooded with calls from hungry Van Halen fans. They wanted to hear songs that put them in the mood, like "Ain't Talkin' 'Bout Love" and "Dance the Night Away." Most of our DJs were also going to the concert and were happy to serve extra helpings of Van Halen tunes. Everyone was feeling good—and about to feel much better.

The station's all-call intercom buzzed and our receptionist frantically announced over the speaker, "Everybody look out the window!" I pulled back my office curtains and peered outside as a pack of motorcycle cops roared to a stop in front of our building, lights spinning and sirens blaring. The police were followed by one…two…three…four long, black limousines. The cops hopped off their bikes and stopped traffic as the limos arrived in succession and parked in front of our studios.

The driver opened the rear door of the first limo and out popped David Lee Roth, flanked by two sleazy women. In the second car was Eddie Van Halen, accompanied by a third babe who carried a giant birthday cake. Now that's full service. Eddie's brother Alex stepped out of the third limo, holding a case of champagne. And finally, bassist Michael Anthony emerged, armed with a huge box of party whistles, poppers and horns.

Van Halen and their ragtag entourage headed straight for the front door of our station like they owned the place. And on this day, they did. Roth led his bandmates into our lobby and stormed through the hallways. As he pushed open the door to the on-air studio, Diamond Dave served notice that Van Halen had come to invade KISW.

David Lee Roth plopped down in the seat at the control board, grabbed the mic from afternoon DJ Gary Crow, and pushed him aside. The other guys in the band presented us with the huge birthday cake and cracked open the case of champagne. Soon corks were popping and everyone was guzzling straight from their own bottle. Champagne glasses were for pussies, I guess. Eddie Van Halen raced around the room spraying people with a penis-shaped squirt gun.

3

I'd officially lost control of my radio station. Roth cranked the studio speakers up to 11 and more people poured into our control room. We were packed together like a subway car at rush hour with our staff, record label reps, photographers and people I didn't even recognize. I found myself pinned against the back wall standing next to Eddie Van Halen. Speechless, I turned to him and sputtered, "What's all this?" Eddie smiled, put his hand on my shoulder and beamed, "We wouldn't miss your birthday!" You hear stories about moments like this—now, I was living one. If the FCC had chosen that moment to inspect our operation, I'd have been fired on the spot and banished to a 10-watt radio station in Blue Balls, Ohio…if I was lucky.

The next two hours were pure bedlam. The word spread around Seattle that Van Halen had taken over KISW, and every rock fan in town was glued to our station. Inside the studio, cake flew, horns blew and shredded paper filled the air. Without any prompting, the strippers jumped up on the console, tore off their bikini tops and started grinding to the beat. Roth and his bandmates played DJ, talked to listeners, and handed out backstage passes to women on the phone who sounded hot. Our phone lines bulged with callers wanting to shoot the breeze with Diamond Dave.

One guy asked a question that all Van Halen fans have long wondered: "Dave, is it true that you have the brown M&Ms removed from the candy bowl in your dressing room?"

Roth replied, "Look, Van Halen likes all colors of M&M's. We don't discriminate. But yeah, our contract requires promoters to remove all brown M&M's, just to make sure they're paying attention. We know if they get that right, we know that everything else is handled. So, it keeps 'em honest."

A woman appealed to Van Halen's serious side, pleading, "Dave, my name is Amanda. I really wish I could see your show tonight. But I'm a quadriplegic and need my wheel-chair. So, I can't go to concerts."

Dave smirked and consoled her, "Sorry to hear that hon. Ya know, I have a special place in my heart for handicapped people. If it weren't for folks like you, I wouldn't have a damn place to park!" With that, Dave howled and punched up the next caller.

The champagne was flowing and the party was rockin' until our sales manager reminded me that we hadn't played any commercials in two hours. Gotta pay the bills. But there was no way that I'd stop this party. So, I suggested we move across the hall while our DJ regained some control. The band, strippers and assorted guests grabbed their champagne and followed me into our production studio. Without missing a beat, the Van Halen party raged on. Roth was on a roll, tossing out funny lines left and right. While nobody noticed, I discreetly started recording the festivities. I had no idea what we'd get, but I couldn't miss this rare opportunity to capture Van Halen in full party mode.

> KISW had been looking for a new, signature voice for our station, someone to inject a rock attitude between songs. Earlier that day, I'd been listening to lots of demo tapes from announcers. But I didn't hear anyone who embodied the rock spirit.

At that moment, I realized that we'd found our announcer. While other radio stations had faceless guys with booming voices, our signature sound would be Van Halen. With tape rolling, we recorded dozens of great cuts from the biggest band in the land. Roth talked about KISW, sang about KISW, and the band even belted out our call letters in four-part harmony. Then Alex Van Halen stepped up to the mic and spoke each letter with echo! K-k-k-k…I-i-i-i…S-s-s-s…W-w-w-w. Never heard anything like that before, or since.

After three hours of full-throttle decadence, Van Halen's manager finally rounded up the band and said, "It's time to go." Dave, Eddie, Alex and Michael left our studios in shambles and stumbled back to their limos, strippers in tow. As the cars pulled away, Roth rolled down his window and yelled, "See ya tonight."

Back inside the station, we weren't sure what had hit us. It looked like a tornado had blown through. Champagne and cake were ground into the carpet. A layer of empty bottles, plates, paper shreds and G-strings were stuck on top. And the walls were sprayed with God knows what. It would be a hard day's night for our cleaning company.

The KISW staff with Van Halen (just before things got out of control)

Chapter 2

I KILLED
PINK FLOYD's PIG

"See how they run like pigs from a gun.
See how they fly, I'm crying."

The Beatles "I Am The Walrus"

Pink Floyd was famous for its astounding live concerts. Their stage show was truly a spectacle, a three-ring circus designed for stadiums. During performances on The Wall Tour, a massive brick wall was constructed between the band and the audience. Then a fighter jet crashed into the stage, demolishing the wall. But the centerpiece of Pink Floyd's concerts was a 40-foot inflatable pig that flew above the crowd.

Roger Waters, the band's spiritual leader, designed the pig and named it Algie. Waters intended to fly the pig over London to celebrate the release of Pink Floyd's breakthrough album, *Animals*. Algie did fly as planned on December 8, 1976. But its maiden voyage was cut short when strong winds snapped the lines and it broke free. Within minutes, the helium-filled pig was spotted by airline pilots, floating 30,000 feet above the English Channel. On that day, Pink Floyd's runaway pig caused all flights in and out of London's Heathrow Airport to be cancelled.

Algie was ultimately recovered and repaired.

Several years later, Pink Floyd's pig took flight again, this time making its American debut over the Seattle skyline. Once again, Algie found trouble.

In 1987, Pink Floyd's final tour performance was scheduled for the Kingdome in Seattle. As the manager of the city's top rock station, I wanted to celebrate this event with something memorable. I called my friend, John Bauer, Pink Floyd's concert promoter. I somehow recruited John to ask Pink Floyd if we could "borrow" their pig and fly it over our station. "Please tell the band's manager that we'd like to anchor Algie on the roof and suspend it over our studios for the week leading up to the concert."

After repeated pleas, Floyd's management company agreed to our request. Bauer cautioned, "Pink Floyd will let you borrow the pig. But there's a caveat. You must promise to deliver it in perfect condition by 12 noon on the day of the show. We'll need several hours to hang Algie from the scaffolding and do some test flights inside the Kingdome."

"That works for us," I agreed. "We promise to return Algie, in perfect shape, by 12 noon."

Several days later, the deflated pig arrived in a wooden six-foot cube. The UPS driver dumped the well-worn crate in the parking lot of our radio station and took off. The packing slip said the box weighed 320 pounds, and it was too large to fit through the front door. So, we used crowbars to unpack the pig, then wrestled it closer to the building. After someone rigged a pulley system, it took four guys to hoist Pink Floyd's pig up three stories to the roof. We spread out the pink fabric, tied down its restraint lines and plugged in the inflation machines. Voila! The pig started filling with air and slowly rose over our building, soaring seventy feet above KISW's studios. Proving that pigs *can* fly, Algie was visible for miles. Local TV cameras flocked to our station to film Pink Floyd's pig. It was the buzz of Seattle for a week. And then my luck ran out.

On the morning of Pink Floyd's concert, I got a 6 a.m. wake-up call from my morning DJ. He only called me at home in emergencies. So I braced myself. "I apologize for calling so early," he said. Then he reluctantly added, "It's still dark outside. But I think the pig is gone."

"What? How can the pig be gone?" I snapped awake.

The DJ answered, "I dunno. I got here about thirty minutes ago, and it was still dark. But when I looked up, I didn't see anything on the roof."

"Shit. Go run outside and check again. It's getting light now." I sat on hold for five nervous minutes, considering all the things that might have happened. If it had broken free again, you'd think that somebody would report seeing a forty-foot pig. After all the media attention Algie had gotten, there was nowhere it could hide.

Our DJ came back to the phone and gasped breathlessly, "Yep, it's gone. The pig must have blown away again. Like in London."

"Damn! Don't say a thing about this on the air. I'm on my way."

I took a two-minute shower, threw on some clothes, and flew out the door. It was now 7 a.m., just five hours before Pink Floyd's stage manager would start hunting me down. My mind raced as I sped toward the radio station. How would I explain to Pink Floyd that I lost their pig?

For those who never saw Pink Floyd's 1987 concert tour, Algie made a grand entrance that drove the crowd wild. Rigging a forty-foot inflatable pig for flight was a complicated process. First, it needed to be inflated inside the concert hall using a combustible mix of oxygen and helium.

Then it was raised up to the roof with long tethers, while roadies balanced on scaffolding towers. The fully inflated pig was then connected to a motorized track that guided its flight path above the crowd.

By 7:45, I was a few blocks from the radio station and driving like a maniac. Straining to see our building up ahead, my worst nightmare was confirmed. No pig. I pulled into the parking lot, leaped out of my car, and headed straight for the back of the building. I scrambled up the ladder that led up to the roof. Sweating bullets as I reached the top, I expected to see nothing but broken straps. But alas, there lay Algie. Looking deflated and humiliated, the pig was just lying in the gravel that covered the rooftop. For the moment, I was elated that the pig was there and not submerged in Puget Sound.

I walked around the rooftop, circling the collapsed pile of pink canvas. Why was it lying here on the roof and not soaring majestically above my station? There had to be some clue as to why it deflated. I lifted up some fabric near Algie's neck and noticed a long shiny object poking out from underneath. I kneeled down to pick it up and discovered a hunting arrow. It looked professional, with a carbon shaft and gold tip. I lifted up the pig a bit higher and saw the problem. The arrow had ripped a gaping hole in the pig's chest. Somebody had shot Algie right in the heart, the bastard.

"Oh shit!" I swore from the rooftop. Someone with serious archery skills had killed Pink Floyd's forty-foot pig, an impressive trophy in any hunter's case. The arrow had torn an L-shaped gash that extended about three feet in each direction. When the air escaped through the nasty hole in its torso, Algie dropped like a sack of wet sand.

It was now 8:30 a.m. My staff scoured the phone book and called a dozen companies, desperate for someone to repair Pink Floyd's pig. But no luck. Time was running out and the pig needed to be stitched up, pronto. Mercifully, we found one parachute maker who agreed to perform immediate surgery. We stuffed the pitiful pig into the station van and quickly slammed the door. Algie completely filled the interior of the van, leaving just enough room for me to drive it. Three guys hopped into another car and followed behind me to the parachute repair shop.

I suspected that the shooter must have come from KZOK-FM, our archrival rock station. Just months before, we defaced their "Not Too Hard. Not Too Soft." billboard. When I say we, it was *me* who added the words "Not Too Good" in spray paint. Was that wrong? After all the grief that we'd caused KZOK, I deserved some retribution. But this time, the timing couldn't be worse.

At 9:30, four of us carried the huge, pink pig into the parachute shop, a dimly lit warehouse. We unfolded it on the floor as the owner inspected the large gash. He was concerned that the edges of the fabric had been shredded, but promised to do his best. To the untrained eye, it wasn't obvious what this mountain of cloth was, and I didn't volunteer any details. Mister Parachute only knew that this was a rush job - no questions asked.

It was now 10:30 and my palms were sweating. While Algie was getting stitched, I called the radio station to retrieve my messages. My assistant told me that Pink Floyd's stage manager had just called to remind me that he needed the pig by noon, if not earlier.

By 11:15, the damage was repaired. But upon close inspection, it was obvious that the parachute maker had covered the gash with a patch, but the colors didn't quite match. The patch was a slightly darker shade of pink. But I was out of time and options. We jammed the mended pig back in the van and thanked the perplexed owner for fixing the hole. I paid him $100 in cash. No, I didn't want a receipt.

We were about forty-five minutes away from the Kingdome. It was raining lightly, which always caused a traffic snarl. This was going to be close. Driving frantically through the wet streets of Seattle, we finally arrived at the backstage gates and were waved through. As our van approached the loading dock, I saw a man standing there with his arms folded, looking pissed. The clock inside the van read 11:59.

I pulled up to the loading dock as the stage manager admonished, "That's cutting it close, man. We'll take it from here."

Pink Floyd's road crew helped us extract the 320 pounds of pig fabric. They were working so quickly that nobody seemed to notice the patch job. As they carted Algie inside the Kingdome, I hopped back in the van and looked back through the rearview mirror. I half expected to see someone chasing after me and yelling about a hole in the pig's chest. But the coast was clear. So, I heaved a sigh of relief and got the hell out of there.

That night, I was excited to see Pink Floyd's concert, but dreaded hearing their song "Pigs." I knew that was Algie's cue to enter the arena and fly over the crowd. Once the spotlight hit the pig, the patch would be clearly visible to 50,000 adoring fans. Would they notice? Would the patch hold under pressure? Or would Algie come crashing down? Moments later, the lights went out and the Kingdome was pitch dark. I knew what was coming next when I heard the opening chords of "Pigs". I tensed as the bright lights illuminated Algie and bathed it in a pink glow. Pink Floyd's famous pig soared over the audience to thunderous applause. The crowd was ecstatic and seemingly too wasted to notice the dark pink patch on Algie's chest.

All the next day I waited nervously for a call from Pink Floyd's manager. I'd spent a sleepless night, dreaming about the tongue lashing that I would get for destroying their precious pig. But the call never came.

In the end, Pink Floyd's pig got shot by an arrow - and I dodged a bullet.

Pink Floyd's pig being raised above our radio station…
before it got punctured

Chapter 3

FLYING THE RED EYE
WITH KEITH RICHARDS

"Pleased to meet you. Hope you guess my name."

Rolling Stones "Sympathy For The Devil"

Airports bustle with activity during the day. But after 10 p.m., they're bleak, deserted tombs. The only people stirring are cleaning crews and road-weary travelers...like me. We wander aimlessly around airports until it's time to line up with other zombie travelers.

It had been a long week of back-to-back meetings in San Francisco. I grew up in the Bay Area, and it still feels like home. But I left it behind years ago to set off on a radio career that bounced me around the country. A few months earlier, I had accepted a job with MTV Networks and moved my family to the suburbs of New York City. More on that later. For now, I just wanted to board the plane and sleep across America.

I rarely fly overnight. But in August of 1993, I booked a red-eye flight to JFK, cashed in some frequent flier miles and upgraded to first class. Just before midnight, I was among the first to board a DC-10 bound for New York. I tossed my bag into the overhead bin and plopped down in my window seat. With nobody to climb over me, I squashed the pillow against the head rest, pulled a blanket over my head, and settled in for an uninterrupted snooze.

At least that was my plan.

As the flight attendants were closing the cabin door, I heard some commotion up front. People were buzzing that a celebrity was getting on board. Oblivious, I closed my eyes and tried to fall asleep. I heard a distant voice say, "Some rock star is getting on the plane." I didn't think much of it. Then, I sensed someone putting a bag under the seat next to me and settling in. I straightened up, turned to my left, opened one eye...and found myself nose-to-nose with Keith Richards. Keith looks a bit ragged on his best days. But at midnight, illuminated by the fluorescent glare of airplane lighting, the man looked like death warmed over. Dressed in a fur coat and clutching a walking stick with a skull on top, the legendary Rolling Stones guitarist shot me a look that said, "Don't fuck with me." I managed a smile and said hello.

I am fortunate to have met many famous musicians. But they don't get any cooler than Keith Richards. If you're a Stones fan, you favor either Mick Jagger or Keith Richards. I'm a Keith guy. He's not just a rock star, he's an icon—an unvarnished genius. The man wrote the book on rock & roll decadence. He is the international spokesman for partying out of bounds. When you Google "party animal," Keith owns the top three positions.

And on this night, Keith Richards lived up to his reputation.

While I was exhausted and ready to sleep across America, Keith was just getting revved up. To him, the night time is the right time. He was wide awake and rarin' to go. I could barely keep my eyes open, but with this rare opportunity, I forced myself to stay awake. How often do you get five-and-a-half uninterrupted hours with a Rolling Stone? The plane's interior lights were off and everyone else on the plane was asleep. Keith and I talked quietly in the darkness, under the glow of a TV monitor playing a Stallone movie. Occasionally I'd drift off only to wake and find Keith staring at me, his arms folded. Like he was insulted that I wasn't keeping him company.

Keith and I chatted about everything from music to American politics to living in Westport, Connecticut (the home of Paul Newman, Martha Stewart and Michael Bolton). As it turned out, Keith and I lived less than ten miles apart. We talked about all things music. Keith's a huge blues fan who reveres the old, black bluesmen and talked about their influence on the Stones' early songs. He is a musician's musician who loves playing live, recording and touring. I got the impression that Keith's more excited about hitting the road than Mick. But whenever I brought up the Rolling Stones, he changed the subject.

I don't want to imply that Keith drank the entire way to New York. But he kept our flight attendant hopping. I lost count of how many drinks he had. The remarkable thing is, it didn't faze him! Richards never seemed drunk. By now, his liver must be pickled.

Keith Richards normally speaks in a loose, sloppy style that can be difficult to understand. Mix in a thick British accent and several stiff drinks and I only caught about 80 percent of what he said. A phrase like "oh, I don't know" sounded like "awwldunno." More than anything, I discovered that Keith is an easygoing guy who doesn't get too stressed over life's obstacles. And there is wisdom in all of those wrinkles. Richards is deceptively sharp and insightful, much smarter than he lets on. He is one of the least pretentious people I've met. It was refreshing to find no star attitude or arrogance. He is who he appears to be, relaxed and spontaneous.

The pilot came on the speaker to announce our descent into New York and that the local time was 7 a.m. Keith laughingly kidded, "I'm a morning person. But I don't keep the same morning hours as you."

As we prepared to land at JFK, Keith turned toward me with a devilish look on his face. He asked, "Would you mind walking off the plane with me? Just until we get into the terminal."

"Of course," I said. "We're pals."

Richards and I waited until everyone got off the plane before heading down the jetway. He gave me a heads up, "There's probably some Stones fans waiting for me. They just want autographs."

"At 7 a.m.?" I asked.

"Yeah. Stones fans have spotters in the airports. When they see me board in San Francisco, they put out the word that I'm flying to New York on flight number such and such. So, stay with me while I finish signing their stuff, then pull me away like we've got to go."

"No problem, Keith," I responded, honored to be his companion and co-conspirator.

As we entered the terminal at JFK, about twelve fans approached Keith, each holding up a guitar for him to sign. He was friendly and accommodating as he talked with each person and signed everyone's guitar. The fans were thrilled to get an autograph from one of the all-time greats. As we reached the last guy in line, Keith took the guitar in his hands and signed his name.

Or so I thought.

When I looked over his shoulder, I noticed that he didn't sign "Keith Richards" on the guitar. He signed *my* name instead!!

Before anyone noticed that their precious instruments had been defaced (and devalued), I hustled Keith away.

"What was that about?" I asked.

Richards laughed. "Look, I will do anything for my fans. But those people just want my autograph so they can sell it online. They're not real fans."

Keith continued, "I know that I'll run into them in airports. So, whenever I travel, I find someone like you and ask them to walk with me into the airport. Then when I get off the plane and people hand me things, I sign my escort's name, not mine." Keith confided, "I learned that one from Mick!"

With that, Keith Richards spotted his driver and headed out into the night, and I haven't seen him since.

I must apologize to those people who are wondering why Keith Richards signed my name on their expensive guitars... in indelible black ink, no less. Your friends will never believe that Keith really did autograph your guitar. But as the song goes, "*You can't always get what you want. But if you try sometimes, you just might find, you get what you need.*"

Chapter 4

WIN A PEARL NECKLACE FROM ZZ TOP

"That's not jewelry she's talkin' about.
It really don't cost that much.
She wanna pearl necklace."

ZZ Top "Pearl Necklace"

When it comes to words with a double meaning, the hands-down winner must be "pearl necklace." Most men recognize "giving her a pearl necklace" as sexual slang for ejaculating on a woman's throat. I am told that this meaning of the phrase is not commonly known among women.

The pearl necklace was immortalized in a song by ZZ Top, released on their 1981 album, *El Loco.* In the summer of that year, "Pearl Necklace" was a hugely popular tune, played in heavy rotation on rock radio stations across America. When that tongue-in-cheek song blasted from car radio speakers, guys would glance at each other and nod knowingly.

ZZ Top's singer/songwriter Billy Gibbons is not shy about writing sexually charged songs. He'd also penned tunes with a similar theme, including "Tush" and "Tube Snake Boogie." So "Pearl Necklace" wasn't much of a stretch. A quick look at the song's lyrics leaves very little to the imagination.

> Rock stations love to play song lyrics that skirt the Federal Communications Commission's (FCC) obscenity rules. But radio must walk a legal tightrope in order to avoid an FCC fine, or worse. Technically, there is nothing illegal about ZZ Top's lyrics. And there is no penalty for a song's hidden meaning.

"She was gettin' bombed and I was gettin' blown away,
And she took it in her hand and this is what she had to say:
A pearl necklace. She wanna pearl necklace."

Rock bands had been getting away with not-so-subtle double entendres for years. Consider this line from Led Zeppelin's "The Lemon Song":

"Squeeze me baby, till the juice runs down my leg. The way you squeeze my lemon, I'm gonna fall right outta bed."

Clearly, Robert Plant wasn't singing about citrus. But he didn't use any of the FCC's seven forbidden words. So, the song was perfectly legal to play on the radio. Likewise, AC/DC's mega-hit "You Shook Me All Night Long" includes the lyric

"She told me to come, but I was already there." Edgy, but perfectly legal.

Bryan Adams once confided that his song "Summer of '69" has nothing to do with the *year* 1969. "I was only thirteen years old then," he admitted. "That song is about a summer I spent getting laid." So think twice the next time you roll down the car windows, crank up your radio, pound the dashboard and sing at the top of your lungs:

"Ohh yeah. Back in the summer of '69... ohh yeah. Me and my baby in '69."

As KISW's program director, I was responsible for everything that came out of the speakers...except for the commercials. Radio ads are the domain of the sales manager.

Program directors (PDs) and sales managers have different agendas and are often at odds. The PD wants to attract an audience, while sales managers bring in the money that pays our salaries. Usually they work together and strike a balance between art and commerce.

Sometimes there's internal friction when clients demand "added value." In return for buying commercials, they want the station to provide something extra, for free. In 1981, we were asked to provide added value for the Shane Company, a national jewelry chain. And boy did we deliver.

You may have heard Shane Company commercials that end with "now you have a friend in the diamond business." They've been running those same, god-awful ads for decades, all stiffly voiced by owner Tom Shane. He reads the script with the passion of a mortician. If you listen closely when Mr. Shane speaks, you can almost hear the stampede of listeners tuning away to another radio station. Shane Company ads are universally mocked by the DJs who must endure them every day. But clients like the Shane Company spent money on our station and money talks. So, we kissed their ass.

I braced myself when our sales manager explained, "The Shane Company wants to sponsor a concert promotion with us. They want our DJs to talk about them on-air." He continued, "Are there any big shows coming to Seattle that we can get them involved in?" I assured our manager that we would help out, but dreaded the idea of associating my station with the Shane Company. Especially as part of a major concert promotion.

So, I needed an idea that preserved KISW's rock image while honoring the Shane Company's request. Throughout that day, I toyed with ways to link a jeweler with a concert. But I came up empty. Then I checked the calendar and noticed that ZZ Top's tour was passing through Seattle the following month. The "Little Ol' Band From Texas" was wildly popular with our listeners, and we'd already planned to make a big deal about their show. But how could I involve the Shane Company? Then it hit me. "Pearl Necklace" was one of the hottest songs on my station. We should do a ZZ Top contest and give away a pearl necklace, courtesy of the Shane Company! I wondered, would the jewelry company get the joke? Or could I slide the pearl necklace reference by them? This could be perfect, if I could get everyone to buy in.

I pitched the idea to our sales manager—and he *loved* it. He immediately phoned his client and put the Shane Company's ad agency on the speaker. Our manager opened the call with, "Our program director, Beau Phillips, has a great idea for a Shane Company promotion. And he's found the perfect concert for you. Go on Beau, tell them."

The Shane Company team eagerly listened as I detailed how my station would promote a contest in which listeners could win a backstage "meet and greet" with ZZ Top. With a straight face, I told the execs that KISW would escort a winner backstage to ZZ Top's dressing room after the show. There, the band members would present the winner with a pearl necklace from the Shane Company.

After a brief pause, I expected to hear a snicker. Or get reprimanded. But I was stunned when nobody flinched about associating the Shane Company with a pearl necklace. "This is exactly what we were looking for!" exclaimed their agent. Apparently, some men are not aware of a pearl necklace's double entendre, including our sales manager and the Shane Company honchos. Turns out that our friends in the diamond business were closet ZZ Top fans, in spite of their naivete about the lyrics. They were thrilled to provide a strand of pearls for the contest winner, and our proposal was roundly endorsed.

It was all I could do to stifle my grin.

Now it was time to have some fun. So, I called ZZ Top's label, Warner Brothers Records, and confirmed the details with the band's management company. Everyone agreed to play along with the gag. KISW's production team created an on-air promo that was saturated with innuendo and double entendre and punctuated with clips from the infamous song. Our listeners were teased with the chance to "come backstage" and "receive a pearl necklace" that would be "hand-delivered by the members of ZZ Top." Our DJs had a blast talking to contestants on-air, who were asked, "Why do you deserve a pearl necklace from ZZ Top?" Their responses were hysterical. The woman who won the contest confessed, "My boyfriend really pulled a boner. He forgot to give me a birthday present. Now, the only gift I want is a pearl necklace."

The night of the concert, I met up with our contest winner and her guest at the concert hall. They were two attractive women in their mid-20s who were dressed to kill. We led them backstage to ZZ Top's dressing room, where they met Billy Gibbons, Dusty Hill and Frank Beard. When the moment was right, Billy said to our winner, "Darlin', why don't you come over here and get down on your knees. I've got your pearl necklace right here." She kneeled down before Billy as he opened the Shane Company box. He removed a beautiful pearl necklace and clasped it around her neck. Pictures were taken and copies were sent to the Shane Company. They were so pleased that the pearl necklace photos were featured in their company newsletter. My sales manager earned his commission. And our listeners were in on the joke. Everybody was a winner.

The moral of this story is: Ladies, when you ask your man for a pearl necklace, be clear about what your heart really desires. I'm told that, given the choice, most women prefer pearls that come from oysters.

With ZZ Top's Billy Gibbons and our contest winner,
about to receive her pearl necklace

Chapter 5

LED ZEPPELIN
MAKES A SPLASH

"Does anyone remember laughter?"

Led Zeppelin "Stairway to Heaven"

When a band heads out on a concert tour, it can last months, sometimes years. Before long, the routine of being on the road gets old and cities all start looking the same. Band members spend countless hours in hotel rooms, and that's when the craziness happens. With plenty of down time in which to amuse themselves, bands often seek out a little mischief.

In 1964, the Beatles' tour passed through Seattle, and killed time by fishing from their windows at the Edgewater Hotel. True to its name, the Edgewater is perched on the water's edge, built on a pier that extends over Puget Sound. At one time, the hotel encouraged guests to fish from the hotel rooms and even stocked a bait shop in the lobby. During their stay, the Beatles did some fishing, but came up empty.

After the fab four's visit, the Edgewater became a local Beatles' landmark, and the hotel took full advantage. The management removed the carpeting from the Beatles' rooms, cut it into small squares and sold the remnants as souvenirs. The Edgewater still maintains a Beatles-themed suite and has hosted several Beatles-related events over the years.

Fast-forward to 1969. The mighty Led Zeppelin was riding high following the release of its debut album. Robert Plant and Jimmy Page became instant rock heroes and set out on their first American tour. Like the Beatles, when the band rolled through Seattle, Led Zeppelin chose to stay at the Edgewater Hotel. And like the Beatles, they fished from their windows. A tale is told in days of old that the band reeled in a small fish, reportedly a mud shark. What happened next is permanently etched in rock lore.

Zeppelin's road manager, Richard Cole, recalls an evening of rock & roll debauchery of mythic proportions. There are several accounts of what actually happened. But everyone agrees that the "mud shark incident" included naked groupies, fish, and body cavities. Cole is quoted in the Led Zeppelin biography *Hammer of the Gods* as saying, "A pretty young groupie with red hair was disrobed and tied to the bed. Led Zeppelin then proceeded to stuff pieces of shark into her vagina and rectum." Accounts vary as to who was responsible. But when a mud shark was hauled into Led Zep's hotel room, it got the attention of the hotel's management. Not surprisingly, the fishing kerfuffle earned the group a lifetime ban from the Edgewater Hotel. Shortly after Led Zeppelin's visit, the Edgewater Hotel closed its bait and tackle shop and ended their "fish from your window" campaign.

One thing is certain. The Beatles made the Edgewater Hotel famous. But Led Zeppelin made it infamous.

In 1977, eight years later, Led Zeppelin returned to Seattle and quietly checked into the Edgewater Hotel in the dead of night...while the city slept.

Wait! What about their lifetime ban?

The hotel manager at the time was named James Blum. He told me, "Somehow Led Zeppelin reserved rooms at the Edgewater and we didn't catch it. There were no computer systems back then. And the band didn't use their real names when booking rooms. So it got past us. Once the band's entourage had checked in, we couldn't just kick them out."

The Edgewater manager hoped this visit would be less eventful. The hotel's reputation took a beating after the mud shark incident, and its image was just recovering. He wanted to avoid any more embarrassment. Blum recalls, "In the spirit of goodwill, I called Led Zeppelin's road manager, Richard Cole. He picked up his room phone, and I welcomed Led Zeppelin back to the Edgewater. I left it at that. Mr. Cole got the message that I knew they were staying at our hotel, despite being banned." More than anything, Blum wanted Richard Cole to know that he'd be watching them.

During Led Zep's return trip, Robert Plant and Jimmy Page didn't fish. But they did make a big splash...five big splashes. On this visit, the band amused themselves by tossing televisions out of their hotel room windows into Puget Sound, then watching them bobbing in the water fifteen feet below.

The former Edgewater manager fills in the details: "Everyone in Led Zeppelin's entourage seemed to be behaving, as far as I could tell. Then, on the morning they were due to check out, I got a call from Celia, the hotel's head housekeeper. I asked her, 'Are the band's hotel rooms still in good condition?' "

"She replied, 'Yes, the rooms are fine. But the TVs are gone.' " Celia spoke with a thick accent. So Blum wasn't sure that he'd heard her correctly and asked the housekeeper to repeat what she'd said.

Celia repeated, "The televisions are missing, in all five rooms."

Blum shook his head and told her, "Stay there. I'm on my way."

The Edgewater manager ran down the hallway and opened the door to one of Led Zeppelin's hotel rooms. "I checked it from top to bottom. She was right, the TV was gone. Just then, a gust of wind blew back the drapes, and I realized the window was open. I walked to the window, pulled back the curtain and looked outside to find not one, but five television sets floating in Puget Sound."

This wasn't the first time that Led Zeppelin had been suspected of tossing televisions. They earned that reputation in the early '70s at the Continental Hyatt House on Sunset Boulevard in Los Angeles, where they reportedly also rode motorcycles down the hallways.

James Blum was speechless. "They did it again!" he muttered. The Edgewater manager walked back toward the lobby and instructed the desk clerk to buzz him when Led Zeppelin came to check out. A few minutes later, Richard Cole walked up to the front desk to settle the band's bill... and Blum was waiting for him. He wanted to come unglued, but James calmly handed a stack of room bills to Zeppelin's manager. The total for all of their rooms was about $3,000. The Edgewater manager recalls, "Richard casually reached into his pocket, pulled out a thick roll of cash and peeled off thirty $100 bills. He pushed the pile of cash across the counter toward me like he was buying a pack of gum."

So far, so good. Blum didn't want to provoke Cole. But he had to address the missing TVs. He swallowed hard and looked Led Zeppelin's manager in the eye. In his most pleasant voice, Blum continued, "Mr. Cole, I must also charge you for those television sets that were thrown out of your hotel room windows."

The road manager smirked and tried to hide his smile. "How many TVs did they toss out?"

"Five," Blum answered. "At $500 per TV, we must charge you an additional $2,500."

Blum expected Richard to go crazy. Instead, Cole chuckled to himself, reached back into his pocket and counted off twenty-five more Ben Franklins. Again, he slid the stack of bills across the counter...like it was nothing.

Meanwhile, the desk clerk was a young guy who'd been watching this transaction. His eyes widened at the sight of Richard Cole's roll and how nonchalant he was about paying a $3,000 tab, in cash. Then piling up another $2,500. Who carries fifty-five $100 bills? Apparently, Zeppelin's manager did. And he still had a few more left in his pocket.

With their hotel bill settled, Cole turned to walk away. Then the young desk clerk worked up the nerve and asked, "Excuse me, Mr Cole. I've heard that Led Zeppelin has a reputation for throwing TVs. But I thought it was BS. Can you tell me, what does it feel like to just toss a TV out of your window?"

Richard Cole stepped back toward the desk, stood in front of the young clerk and replied, "Kid, there are some things in life that you've got to experience for yourself." With that, Cole reached back into his pocket and unrolled five more crisp $100s. He laid the cash on the counter, pushed them across to the clerk and said, "Here you go mate, go toss a TV courtesy of Led Zeppelin!"

Led Zeppelin's entourage has not returned to the Edgewater Hotel since then. And I doubt that the hotel management saved the carpet squares from their rooms. But the legend lives on.

Chapter 6

ERIC CLAPTON'S
TEARS IN HEAVEN

"I must be strong, and carry on,
'Cause I know I don't belong here in heaven."

Eric Clapton "Tears in Heaven"

In the pantheon of rock gods, Eric Clapton is revered as one of the greatest songwriters and guitarists of our generation. But in 1991, we got a sense of Eric Clapton the mortal. As a father, he faced the hardest test a man can bear, dealing with the death of his 4-year-old son, Conor.

Ironically, Eric Clapton had recently decided to be a better father for the first time in his life. He regretted that he wasn't closer to his young son and made efforts to change that. Conor lived in Milan with his mother, Lory Del Santo, Clapton's ex-girlfriend. After she and Clapton split up, he wanted to spend time with his boy while they were visiting New York. The day before Conor's death, father and son went to the circus on Long Island. It was their first time alone, together. After dropping Conor back home that evening, Eric told Lory, "I now understand what it means to be a father."

Clapton had planned to take his son to the Central Park Zoo the following day. Lory was getting ready in the bathroom while Conor ran around the 53rd-floor apartment playing hide and seek with his nanny. What nobody realized was that the sliding door to the balcony had been left open after it was cleaned by the housekeeper. According to police, it was unprotected by a window guard. The boy, who was not in the room during the cleaning, darted past the housekeeper and through the open door and fell to his death. The panic-stricken nanny dashed to the bathroom and told Lory, "Conor's gone!".

Eric Clapton was just blocks away when Lory called him with the horrific news. He shared his reaction years later with interviewer Larry King. "I didn't rush at all. I slowed down. It was almost as if I was trying to stop time. So I put the phone down. And I remember walking very, very slowly from where I was staying to their apartment, about five blocks away. I'm going over it in my mind, thinking this hasn't happened, almost like I was trying to freeze time. When I got there, I saw paramedics and police cars and thought this looks like it's true."

Grieving after just starting to bond with his son, Clapton summoned the courage to visit Conor at the funeral home, "to say good-bye and apologize for not being a better father." That's when he received a letter that Conor had written to his father just before he died. Lory revealed in a television interview, "The baby had learned to write a few words, and he said to me, 'Oh Mummy, I want to write a letter to Daddy, what shall I write?' I told him, 'Well, write "I love you." Conor wrote that down and sent the letter to his dad." Lory continued, "After Conor died, Eric and I flew to London for the funeral. I was there when Eric received his mail just after the ceremony. He opened it up and it was Conor's letter. That is a moment I cannot forget."

As he often had, Clapton turned to music to ease his pain. Somehow, he mustered the strength to deal with Conor's death and spoke to his late son in a song. Clapton dug down deep and composed the heart-wrenching ballad "Tears In

Heaven," a father's musings about reuniting with his son in heaven. To his fans in the late '60s, Clapton was referred to as God. In that song, Clapton seemed to touch God in the way he accepted his son's death with such grace.

"Would you hold my hand if I saw you in heaven?
Would you help me stand if I saw you in heaven?"

In 1992, just months after the tragedy, Eric Clapton embarked on a world tour. He performed "Tears In Heaven" in concert every night. As a father, I cannot fathom his strength and courage. Writing that song must have been excruciating. But playing it over and over, in public, must have been a recurring nightmare. Or maybe it was therapeutic.

When Eric Clapton's tour hit town, I wanted to find an appropriate way to celebrate his concert appearance, not the typical tenth-caller-ticket-giveaway contest. It was important to honor Clapton's show, but not sensationalize it. How could we let Clapton know that we shared his pain? How could we thank him for performing his song for fans while he was still grieving?

"Tears in Heaven" first appeared on the soundtrack album for the movie *Rush*. A few months later, Eric Clapton performed the song in a small theater in Windsor, England, where it was recorded by MTV for his *Unplugged* album. The album and song combined to win six Grammy awards including Record of the Year, Album of the Year and Best Rock Song. The album reached number one and sold more than ten million copies in the U.S. alone.

At our weekly managers meeting, I suggested, "Let's do something special at the concert when Clapton plays 'Tears in Heaven.' Something that's meaningful and shows respect." We created a plan to pass out free, commemorative lighters at the concert. We would hand one to each fan as they entered the concert hall. When Clapton performed "Tears in Heaven," the crowd would honor Conor by holding up their lighters in a silent tribute. On this night, 20,000 fans would comfort Eric Clapton without saying a word.

My team was on board, so I reached out to a promotion manager at the Bic corporation. When I explained the backstory of "Tears In Heaven," he was touched. I laid out our plan and asked his company to donate lighters for fans at Eric Clapton's concert. Bic was happy to oblige and shipped 20,000 Bic lighters to us, at no charge, because it was the right thing to do.

In the weeks leading up to Clapton's show, our DJs encouraged listeners to grab a Bic lighter as they entered the concert. Then, we instructed them, "When you hear the first notes of 'Tears In Heaven,' turn on your lighter and hold your flame high. But don't make a sound. Don't clap or cheer. Just raise your lighter high in the air and silently pay tribute."

We had Clapton's logo silk-screened onto the 20,000 lighters, packed them into dozens of satchel bags, and dispatched our staffers to the concert hall. Our team dispersed and passed out free Bic lighters at every entrance to the arena. As we handed them to fans, we reminded them what to do. After an hour, all of the lighters had been distributed. We stashed our empty satchels and headed inside for the show.

Clapton took the stage and smiled to the crowd as he opened with his blistering hit, "Forever Man." The place went wild. Clapton nodded to the crowd and seemed to feel at ease. Maybe touring helped him heal. About thirty minutes into the show, his band left the stage and Clapton set down his

Fender Stratocaster. A heavenly blue light bathed the stage as he took a seat on a stool. He picked up his acoustic guitar, and everyone in the arena sensed what song was coming next. The anticipation was chilling as Clapton drew a deep breath and began playing the opening guitar notes of "Tears in Heaven." As I'd hoped, the concert hall went totally quiet. Pin-drop quiet. Then, in unison, all 20,000 fans silently raised their lighters above their heads.

Clapton, with his eyes closed and head bowed, played a few more notes. Then, when he didn't hear any response from the audience, he looked up from his guitar. He appeared stunned and paused for a few seconds to take it all in. Usually, a performer has lights shining in his face and can't see beyond the first ten rows. But on that night, Eric Clapton saw a sea of raised lighters stretching all the way to the back of the arena. He had to know that this silent offering was a show of respect for his late son.

Time seemed to stop as everyone in the audience shared a real moment, a genuine connection with Eric Clapton, the father. He was clearly moved and stared at the crowd for about twenty seconds before lowering his head and resuming the song. Looking around, I saw many fans watching the stage with tears in their eyes. It seemed that Clapton felt it too. His voice quivered as he sang the poignant line to his late son, *"Would you know my name, if I saw you in heaven?"*

Whenever I hear "Tears in Heaven," I remember that profound experience. And I know there are 20,001 others who feel the same.

Chapter 7

TUXEDO TOM PETTY

"Fashion fades, only style remains the same."

Coco Chanel

In 1979, Tom Petty had rock fans in the palm of his hand. Radio stations across America couldn't get enough of his brilliant album *Damn The Torpedoes,* and the airwaves were flooded with tasty songs like "Don't Do Me Like That," "Refugee," and "Here Comes My Girl." In no time, the *Torpedoes* album went platinum and catapulted Petty from playing club gigs to selling out huge arenas.

With one million albums under their belt, Tom Petty and the Heartbreakers hit the road. They were scheduled to play at Seattle's legendary Paramount Theater in late December of '79, toward the end of the tour. The theater was an elegant, vintage venue with a gilded lobby, ornate chandeliers and red velvet seats. In other words, perfectly suited for a rock concert. It was an unusually small venue compared to the rest of Petty's other tour stops. In most cities, the Heartbreakers were performing in 12,000-seat arenas. The Paramount, with a seating capacity of only 3,000, would be an intimate show by comparison.

I pulled my staff together to brainstorm ideas for the concert. When everyone was assembled, I addressed the team. "Petty's show is December 29th . It's our final show of the decade and we want rock fans to look their best. So, let's end the '70s with a bang and make it memorable!"

I pitched my staff on doing a tuxedo concert for Tom Petty. "Instead of giving away station T-shirts, let's raise the bar and give every ticket holder a tuxedo jacket...free! Men *and* women. What a sight for Petty to see a theater full of rock fans wearing tux coats!" One of our staffers wasn't convinced. "The show is already sold out. Petty is so hot right now, that offering free tux coats will just drive people insane."

> I'd filed away the crazy notion of staging a "tuxedo concert" by giving every concertgoer a KISW-branded tuxedo jacket. Free. I was sure that rock fans would proudly wear these coats around town, promoting our station. But I just never found the right opportunity. And I didn't have the budget to buy thousands of tuxedo coats. So I shelved the idea, but I never forgot about it. Maybe we could try it now. The timing was perfect!

"That's the idea," I exclaimed. "I want this show to be an 'I was there' experience that people will talk about for years. Giving away tuxedo jackets will make it special."

Now, all we had to do was *find* 3,000 tuxedo jackets.

Our promotions director called a few places and finally found a large formal wear company that agreed to meet with us. As luck would have it, Brocklind's Tuxedos was a local company that manufactured and sold formal wear around the world. They dealt in tremendous volume.

We spent a half hour with Jerry, the company president, explaining our plan for a tuxedo concert. He nodded and listened politely. But I could tell he'd never heard of Tom Petty and couldn't grasp why we'd give away free tux jackets.

If nothing else, I learned something about the formal wear business. Jerry explained, "When tuxedo jackets go out of style, we scrap them. As lapels get wider or thinner, or the number of buttons change, the coats are worthless to us. So we either incinerate them, write them off as a tax loss, or donate the tuxes to marching bands." I took that as an encouraging sign. It sounded like this company had lots of outdated coats that they wanted to ditch. And I didn't care about the lapels or buttons. I had my opening and put it out there. "We'd like to take 3,000 tuxedo jackets off your hands."

The Brocklind's president didn't flinch when I mentioned that I needed 3,000 coats. So I kept going. "We don't have any money to pay for them. Would you be willing to donate the tux jackets to our radio station for the concert event?" I'm sure he thought I was nuts.

"Let me get this straight," he smiled. "You have no money to spend? And you want me to *give* you 3,000 tuxedo jackets—for nothing!?"

"Technically yes," I pressed on. "But the jackets are worthless to you anyway, and you'd be donating them to support this wonderful event. I have an idea how to make it worth your while." I half expected the tux company president to kick me out of his office. Instead, he sat back in his chair and stared out of the window. He seemed to be considering my request. After a minute or so, he turned back toward me and asked, "Okay, so what can you do for me in return?"

"Sir," I replied, "I've taken the liberty of drafting a barter proposal that offers Brocklind's free radio commercials on our station in exchange for the coats."

"Actually, that might work," he mulled. "We rent a lot of formal wear during wedding and prom season. We could use some advertising." Smelling blood in the water, I poured it on. "Exactly. And my radio station is the perfect way to reach your customers." He was nodding again. So, I pushed my luck further. "Assuming we can come to an agreement, can you deliver 3,000 coats by December 15th?"

"That shouldn't be a problem," he said. "We've got a warehouse full of tuxedo jackets. But they come in all different sizes and colors. Do you care if they all match?"

"Not at all," I answered. "This is a rock concert, not a wedding." As far as I was concerned, the funkier the better. We weren't trying to make a fashion statement.

"Okay," said Jerry. "I can give you an assortment of tux coats, tails and smoking jackets. They come in every color of the rainbow. Some are beautiful and hardly worn. Others look pretty tacky. You'll get canary yellow, lime green, aqua, black, fire-engine red, plaid and blue velvet. Mostly the less popular styles and colors. A little bit of everything. But they're all gently used and in great condition."

I kept a poker face. But inside I was doing backflips. We came to terms with the tuxedo company for 3,000 jackets, valued at just $5 each. In return, KISW would provide $15,000 in commercials, about 500 free ads. It was a helluva deal for everyone. The tuxedo company was happy to get free radio ads for jackets it didn't want. And we were thrilled to score 3,000 tuxedo jackets for zero dollars.

"I hope you've got a big storage room," Jerry advised. "If you stack 3,000 jackets in a pile, they would probably fill a fifteen- by fifteen-foot room to the ceiling."

Gulp. I arranged for them to ship the jackets straight to our printer who would silk-screen Tom Petty's logo on the breast pocket of each coat. On the back, they screened KISW's logo. And best of all, MCA Records, Tom Petty's label, paid the printing bill.

The word spread quickly about our tuxedo concert, and the local TV stations called to get permission to film the festivities. On the day of the concert, fans lined up early around the Paramount Theater. Everyone wanted to make sure to get a tuxedo jacket, even though we had enough for everyone.

Inside the theater, the lobby was jammed with three enormous piles of jackets. The tuxedo coats had been sorted into three equal stacks: 1,000 Medium, 1,000 Large and 1,000 X-Large. As promised, there was a wild assortment of colors and styles. Some of the jackets were elegant while others looked like they were made from cheap hotel curtains. Some were formal black tails and white dinner jackets. Others were so ugly, they were cool.

The theater manager approached me and confided, "There's a special box of tux jackets for you in my office. They were sent by the tux company president especially for this occasion." I followed him back to the theater office and opened the box. Inside were twelve brand new velvet smoking jackets. They were a beautiful deep blue color with the Petty and KISW logos silkscreened in gold ink. I had a plan for those special jackets and stashed them away backstage.

As fans came through the front doors of the Paramount, they called out their sizes and our staff tossed them coats. Then, fans were steered back outside to get back in line. It would have taken hours to let 3,000 people try on different jackets. So fans got what they got and even traded coats with other folks in line. Every Petty fan seemed thrilled to get a tux jacket, including Tom's female fans. Tonight, everyone was here to celebrate the last show of the decade in style.

Outside, the line of tuxedo-wearing fans was a sight to behold. People stood along the side of the theater and the line stretched for blocks. Every fan was decked out in a tuxedo jacket, and they were all taking pictures of each other. Television news copters hovered overhead, filming the long line of formally dressed rock fans.

As Petty fans filed into the Paramount, the theater, with its smattering of yellow, purple, red, and turquoise, looked like a Jackson Pollock painting. I stood in the last row of the balcony, admiring our accomplishment. Then, I headed backstage, grabbed the blue velvet jackets and took the elevator up to the band's dressing room. Petty's road manager led me inside, and I saw Tom and the Heartbreakers stretched out on couches around the room. Petty was dressed in black jeans and a western-styled shirt. He was strumming his 12-string Rickenbacker guitar while the Heartbreakers' drummer kept time on a folding chair. I cleared some space on a nearby table and laid out the crushed velvet coats. Tom and the other guys gathered around, and Petty asked, "What are these?"

"Well, tonight is December 29th," I answered. "This is our final concert of the decade, and my radio station wanted to do it up in style. So we cut a deal for 3,000 tuxedo jackets, printed your logo on them, and handed out a free tux jacket to everyone in the audience."

Petty looked startled and asked, "Wait, what? Are you saying that everybody in the crowd is wearing one of these?"

"Yep, probably blue jeans and a tux jacket."

The band members looked at one another and laughed. "Are you shitting me? How cool!"

I pointed to the blue jackets and offered, "We had these coats made just for you. They are brand new, Palm Beach smoking jackets made of crushed velvet." While some of the 3,000 jackets looked god-awful, these were beautiful. I handed a coat to Petty and everyone in his band (and saved one for myself). The guys loved their tux jackets and preened in front of each other. Some people thought I was nuts to outfit every fan in a tuxedo jacket. But seeing the band's reaction made it all worthwhile.

It was about five minutes until showtime. So, I said my goodbyes and headed for the door. I looked back and threw the Hail Mary: "We'd really love it if you guys would wear your coats onstage tonight." I'm not sure that they heard me because Petty and his bandmates were busy admiring themselves in the mirror.

I headed back into the theater to watch the show. I couldn't wait to see Petty's reaction when he looked into the audience and saw a multicolored sea of jackets. Moments later, the house lights dimmed, the curtains parted, and Tom Petty took the stage, kicking off our "end of the decade" show. Tom strolled to the center microphone, shielded his eyes from the spotlights, and gazed over the crowd. Shaking his head in disbelief, he said to the audience, "Holy shit. You guys look fuckin' great!" Three thousand tuxedo-clad fans jumped to their feet and yelled like crazy. But I was disappointed that Petty and the Heartbreakers weren't wearing their blue velvet coats. They were still dressed in the same clothes they wore backstage. I was bummed, but suppressed my disappointment and settled in to enjoy the show.

Petty played for nearly two hours, and his fans stood the entire time. They danced in the aisles, sang along, and never took off their jackets. When the set ended, Petty and the Heartbreakers left the stage. As usually happens, the crowd continued clapping, hoping the band would return for an encore. The stage was dark. But I could see movement and flashlights waving, which meant that the band was coming back on stage. When the lights came up again, Tom Petty and his bandmates were wearing their velvet jackets! I was thrilled that they saved this surprise for their encore. Tuxedo Tom smiled as he stepped up to the mic and tugged at his lapels. "I heard this show was formal," he joked. The crowd went nuts as Petty tore into his hit "Refugee" before calling it a night.

I stood in the lobby after the show, watching the crowd file out of the Paramount. Fans were still jazzed and showing off their tux coats. As we'd hoped, people coveted their souvenir jackets. For years, I saw fans walking through concerts wearing our tuxedos. And the legacy lives on. Tom Petty/KISW tuxedo jackets still come up for sale online, thirty-five years after the concert that ushered out the decade.

Chapter 8

AC/DC GETS DIRTY

"If you think it's easy doin' one night stands,
Try playin' in a rock roll band.
It's a long way to the top if you wanna rock n' roll."
AC/DC "It's A Long Way To The Top"

People laughed at my radio station for playing AC/DC. Program directors at other rock stations would scoff, "It's just 'cock rock' for mouth-breathing, knuckle-dragging teenage boys." True enough. But we knew that AC/DC's appeal spread far beyond that.

KISW made no excuses for playing rock music that had power and passion. And AC/DC churned out a primal rhythm like nobody's business. In 1978, we first felt the groin-tingling thrust of their *Powerage* album and saw the band's potential for greatness. Over the years, we enjoyed a tight relationship with the band, its managers and label, Atlantic Records.

In the late '70s, rock was dormant, lying in wait. It seemed that music fans had been lulled into submission by glitz, disco, and saccharine bon bons like "You Light Up My Life." Bands like the Eagles, Dire Straits, and the Cars politely carried the rock flag. But a seismic shift was starting to rumble deep in the earth's core.

On a rare sunny afternoon in Seattle, Steve Slaton and I visited a local Kmart and headed straight for the record department. Steve was our station's music director and a wildly popular rock DJ in town. Together, we chose the music that KISW played. Steve and I met weekly with promotional reps from every record label and listened to their latest batches of music. We loved to find exciting new songs to showcase on-air.

In recent years, radio's musical spirit of adventure has been neutered. Broadcasting companies are now run by soulless accountants who've drained the creative juices from stations. The wonder of music discovery has given way to tedious repetition. But I digress.

Steve and I were flipping through vinyl albums in the import section when we came upon an AC/DC album that we'd never seen before. The record was called *Dirty Deeds Done Dirt Cheap*. The one and only copy in the bin. We were very familiar with the band's music catalog. But we'd never even heard of *Dirty Deeds*. Steve and I later learned that this album was released in 1976, but only in Australia. It was never available for sale in America. We looked at each other like we'd found the missing link. This seemed like a rare find. So we bought the Australian import album and raced back to KISW for a listen.

It was a long way to the top for AC/DC, and the band went through hell to get there. Just as the group started to taste success, their lead singer drank himself to death. The band's breakthrough album, *Highway To Hell,* catapulted AC/DC to stardom while Bon Scott died alone in his car. Losing its singer sent the band into a tailspin. Understandably, AC/DC took time to regroup. The band was devastated by Bon's death, but chose to carry on with a new singer. After a fairly brief search, the "bad boys from down under" announced their new gravel-throated front man, Brian Johnson.

Meanwhile, rock fans were hungry for more AC/DC tunes. Our station had played their songs to death and didn't have anything fresh to play. We were hoping to find a good song or two on this album. So, we closed the door to Slaton's office and excitedly set the needle down on side 1, cut 1 of *Dirty Deeds Done Dirt Cheap.*

Four minutes later, we stared at each other, dumbfounded. The album's title song knocked us out. We restarted the record and listened for another thirty-eight minutes. When the *Dirty Deeds* album ended, the speakers were glowing red. Steve and I couldn't believe our luck. We had unearthed a rare AC/DC gem that had never been played on American radio. Nobody else even knew about it!

Slaton started talking up the album during his evening show and played songs from *Dirty Deeds* in heavy rotation. He dug deeper into the album and treated our listeners to Bon Scott snarling through songs like "Jailbreak," "Big Balls," "Ride On" and "Squealer." The album was loaded with tasty morsels that our listeners devoured. *Dirty Deeds Done Dirt Cheap* quickly became the most requested album on our station, and we could feel AC/DC's undeniable surge.

Word got out to rock stations around the country that KISW had discovered a great AC/DC album, featuring Bon Scott at his fiery best. Many stations tried to find copies of the album, but couldn't. We must have found the only imported copy! So when they called about our success with *Dirty Deeds*, we helped them out and sent tapes of *Dirty Deeds* to stations in L.A., New York, Chicago, Philly and other cities. Soon, the Australian wildfire spread across America.

Those people who thought we were crazy for playing AC/DC weren't laughing now.

Before long, I got a call from Judy Libow, Atlantic Records' VP of Rock Promotion. While AC/DC is on her label, Judy had never heard of the *Dirty Deeds* album either. It was never sold in America, so it was completely off her radar. Now that AC/DC had a new groundswell of interest, Atlantic wanted to get their hands on *Dirty Deeds* and release it in the U.S. Once they did, *Dirty Deeds Done Dirt Cheap* shot up the *Billboard* magazine charts to #3, several years after it was originally released in Australia.

The sad irony is that Bon Scott's voice was known, but he wasn't. Bon died right before AC/DC hit it big in America. So, his legend only intensified after his death. Bon Scott's fans knew nothing about him, and they would never see him perform again.

Or would they?

I was approached by a husband-and-wife team who owned the rights to the film *AC/DC: Let There Be Rock*. I'm embarrassed to say that I'd never even heard of this movie. The couple had read about our success with AC/DC and asked KISW to help promote the film. *Let There Be Rock* was booked for a limited, two-week engagement at a local theater. The couple wanted to play the film as many times as possible during its two-week theater run to gauge if the film had commercial potential to run nationally. Their timing could not have been better. Coming off the success of *Highway To Hell* and now *Dirty Deeds*, AC/DC was white hot.

The couple arranged for a private showing for Slaton and me. We learned that *Let There Be Rock* was filmed in Paris in December of 1979, just two months before Bon Scott's death. Steve and I had never seen Bon Scott perform, so we were thrilled at the chance to enjoy him live, in concert. In a word, the band was blistering. The French crowd roared its approval as Bon Scott ripped off his shirt and worked the stage. Guitarist Angus Young hammered out hard, grinding solos and—as was customary—he pulled down his knickers to moon the crowd. AC/DC was riveting onstage. When projected on a large movie theater screen, the band loomed larger-than-life. I knew that our listeners would be hungry for this film and offered the full support of our radio station. Our DJs hosted showings around the clock and promoted the movie relentlessly. It was a must-see for any AC/DC fan.

After the first week, the husband and wife called me with a status report. They were ecstatic. "The response to *Let There Be Rock* has been overwhelming! Ticket sales were better than we'd even dreamed. Almost every show was sold out!" Then came the real kicker: "*Let There Be Rock* sold more tickets at that theater in its first week than *Star Wars!*" That record stood for years.

After two weeks of raging success in Seattle, *Let There Be Rock* was released to movie houses across America, with similar results. The concert film even spawned a DVD package, complete with a collector's tin, concert pictures, a souvenir guitar pick, and a 32-page booklet.

With AC/DC fans satisfied for the moment, we eagerly waited for the band to release its first new material with Brian Johnson, the iconic album *Back In Black*. When the record finally arrived, it was well worth the wait. Slaton and I drove to Vancouver, B.C., for opening night of AC/DC's Back In Black Tour, their first concert in North America featuring the new singer. Nobody had heard of Brian Johnson, and we were curious to see how he'd fill Bon Scott's big shoes.

Peter Mensch, AC/DC's manager, invited us to watch the show from the soundboard. As the lights went down, Peter leaned over and winked, "Watch this." A single spotlight shone down on the stage as an enormous brass bell appeared, suspended twenty feet in the air. Slowly, it descended, stopping four feet above the stage. AC/DC's new singer stepped out of the darkness, and the rock world got their first glimpse of Brian Johnson. He raised a huge mallet overhead and slammed it down on the bell. Then slowly, he hit it again, and again. Angus Young's now familiar guitar riff slid in under the ringing bell as the throbbing bass and drum beats built to a crescendo. The classic song "Hell's Bells" made its debut...and sent fans into a frenzy.

After the show, Slaton and I headed backstage to interview the band. We sat down for an exclusive chat with Brian, Angus, and his brother Malcom Young, AC/DC's rhythm guitarist. They look like enormous titans onstage. But in person, the band members were shorter than I expected, each standing about five feet six.

AC/DC didn't grant many interviews. So, we savored this private hour with the band. Afterward, Atlantic Records took our recorded conversation, pressed it on a vinyl album and distributed copies to rock stations around the country.

AC/DC plays balls-to-the-walls in concert. Backstage they looked exhausted, drenched in sweat. The guys slumped forward in folding chairs, towels wrapped around their necks and hair matted to their faces. We sat in a circle, surrounding a large tub of Heinekens. Angus Young drank a cup of hot tea while the rest of us pulled bottles from the ice. But we couldn't find a bottle opener. The band was hot and thirsty, but there was no opener in sight.

Then Brian Johnson did one of the most extraordinary things I've ever witnessed. He said, "No problem mates," and lifted the beer bottle up to his face. He tilted it back, placed the cap next to his eyeball, and pulled the bottle down sharply. The cap flew off and fell to the floor. Johnson had removed the bottle cap using only his eye socket! My jaw dropped. Brian smiled, "That trick comes in handy when I'm out drinkin' with my boys." Miraculously, Johnson wasn't bleeding. In fact, he proceeded to open everyone's beer, like it was nothing.

Now that's one tough dude who's been down the highway to hell.

AC/DC is one of the top-selling bands of all time. They rank third in all-time rock album sales, behind only Led Zeppelin and Pink Floyd. AC/DC can sell out a 60,000-seat stadium concert on a moment's notice…anywhere in the world. I'd like to think that a lucky find in a record bin may have had something to do with that success.

Chapter 9

STING SUCKS YOU IN

"I want my MTV."

Sting/Dire Straits "Money For Nothing"

In the mid-90s, I left radio behind and moved to New York to be the head of marketing for VH1. The cable music channel was MTV's older, dysfunctional brother. It was aimed at "MTV graduates," music fans who'd outgrown teen pop. Over the years, VH1 had tried many different approaches. When I arrived, VH1 was a hodgepodge of lame music videos, WKRP reruns, and Gallagher's watermelon-smashing comedy specials. Nothing was working, and the network had zero credibility. Clearly, it was time for a facelift.

We started by dumping the sitcoms and comedy specials. VH1's management team made a commitment to being a true music channel and adopted the handle "Music First." With a slate of fresh, new shows in development, it was time to tell the world. I worked with our ad agency to develop a TV campaign that celebrated the *new* VH1. Our plan was to recruit huge music stars to re-launch our channel. With their endorsement, we'd spread the word that VH1 had been reborn as a cool music channel. Most rock stars would never consider appearing in a TV commercial, especially an endorsement spot. But MTV Networks had tremendous clout. So, our team aimed for the top and contacted three of the hottest stars at the time: Madonna, Sting and Sheryl Crow. Calls were made, favors were called in, and strings were pulled. Within a few days, all three stars agreed to appear in our TV campaign, at no charge.

Our agency created a campaign called "VH1 sucks you in." Each TV spot would show average people watching a music video before they suddenly got pulled, literally, into the scene. The viewer would be transported into the artist's music video and suddenly appear alongside the artist. Each commercial would end with Sheryl, Madonna or Sting teasing, "The new VH1. It will suck you in."

To merge someone's image into the music video required a special CGI effect. So, we used what was then the latest blue-screen technology, the same technique used in the movie *Forrest Gump* to make Tom Hanks appear to shake hands with Richard Nixon.

We filmed three individual commercials in three different locations. First, we flew Sheryl Crow to New York City and filmed her spot in a Manhattan loft. I arrived early and met her in a small trailer that was parked outside our shooting location in Chelsea. Sheryl was down-to-earth and easy to talk with. She eagerly listened to the plan for our commercial as a stylist curled her hair. We walked up to the loft with Sheryl's trusty golden retriever by her side. The commercial featured Crow's video for "All I Wanna Do," the song that put Crow on the map. In our commercial, a woman is watching the video while jogging on a treadmill. Then, all of a sudden, our jogger magically appears in the video alongside Sheryl Crow. The spot ends with Sheryl curled up on a couch, wearing the same outfit from the video, saying, "The new VH1, it will suck you in." Perfect, it's a wrap. Sheryl was a sweetheart to deal with, without a hint of attitude.

Two days later, Madonna filmed her commercial on a cold evening in lower Manhattan. Enter the drama queen. Her management company challenged us at every turn. "C'mon," we implored, "This is a simple ad, not *Gone With The Wind*." Our TV spot was set to Madonna's hit "Take A Bow." She was only required to sit in a car parked at the curb as her date got out to use an ATM. She cooperated, but not before playing every diva card in the deck. The "Material Girl" insisted that we retrieve the exact dress that she wore in the video, even though it was a common black dress that would be covered by her coat. Madonna's scene was a single shot that lasted about five seconds. But that didn't stop her handlers from making eye-roll worthy demands. We finally said no when Madonna insisted that VH1 fly in her hairdresser from Europe.

Once she arrived on the set with her entourage, Madonna was swept into a trailer and remained hidden inside. She didn't speak with anyone, and we were told not to speak to her. Some say that you don't want to get stuck in a small space with Madonna. Believing that, I stayed ten feet away and had no direct contact with her, which was just as well. Once the cameras rolled, Madonna emerged from her cocoon and had a lot of fun with our tagline. She nailed the "suck you in" line and sold it convincingly. If only we'd saved those provocative outtakes.

With two commercials in the can, our attention turned to Sting. The former chief of the Police was making a movie in a deserted castle in northern England. Sting agreed to meet us on the set of his movie *The Grotesque*. To pull this off, I'd have to fly to London, drive a few hours to a remote location, and film our spot between movie scenes. We had no plan B. So I booked a red-eye flight from New York to London and arrived at Heathrow airport at 6 a.m. I hired a driver, and we headed toward the castle on the North Sea for my rendezvous with Sting.

On this beautiful, crisp morning, we drove through the English countryside as the sun warmed the earth and steam rose from the fields. After miles of driving on narrow, bumpy roads, I arrived on location. The film crew was setting up their gear in a church about 500 yards from the castle. This grey stone building was once a monastery, built in the 1700s. It had endured brutally harsh weather over the centuries and lost most of its roof. But the church had a majestic look, with no glass or doors—only rectangular-shaped holes in the thick, stone walls. Its 300 years of history would soon include the filming of a TV commercial starring one of England's greatest stars.

In the film, Sting played a character named Fledge, a butler who seduced most of the female cast. *The Grotesque* **pretty much describes the movie's box office performance. It quickly disappeared from theaters. I never saw the film, and apparently I wasn't alone.**

We patiently waited for Sting inside the church and decided to film him standing at the altar. I was standing in front of the church talking with the film crew when Sting came into view. Dressed in a dark blue topcoat, he walked along the dirt road that led to the castle. Even from a distance, it was evident that Sting had a self-assured grace. He approached us with a welcoming smile and extended his hand. We shook hands and led him into the church. Sting has an undeniable aura and exuded a serene presence, probably thanks to his practice of Transcendental Meditation and yoga. He was so calm that it's hard to imagine his legendary fights with bandmates in the Police.

Sting listened intently to our plan as he changed into the clothes he wore in the "Fields of Gold" video. "I'll do whatever you want," Sting offered. "I've got about thirty minutes, so I'm ready when you are." I couldn't help but flash back on the Madonna experience a few days earlier, when everything was a problem. Sting couldn't have been more gracious and accommodating.

The film crew fussed with the lighting and camera placement. Because Sting had come from the movie set, he didn't need any makeup. Without any drama or pretense, he stood in front of the camera and stared confidently into the lens. As the cameras started to roll, we all shared an overpowering spiritual experience inside that old church. The sun had risen just high enough for shafts of sunlight to pour through the openings in the stone walls. The effect was surreal, and we wanted to capture that lighting on film. Quickly, the crew repositioned Sting on the altar as the videographer filmed him from knee level, shooting upward. The morning sun cast a warm glow on Sting's shoulders that gave him an ethereal, spine-tingling presence. When backlit, his blond hair gave the illusion he was wearing a golden halo. Sting looked regal, a true rock god.

We recorded four or five takes, and Sting delivered the "suck you in" line perfectly each time. An assistant from the movie set tapped me on the shoulder and announced that Sting was needed back on the The Grotesque set. So, we said our goodbyes and rushed the tape back to New York. Our producers added the finishing touches, and our three "suck you in" ads debuted on the season premiere of Seinfeld.

Seeing the "sucks you in" commercials gave me a sense of pride. Getting three superstars to endorse the channel was a huge accomplishment. It's hard to say if the ads were effective. But music fans got the message that VH1 finally had a purpose. In the months that followed, the channel introduced fresh, new shows that took viewers Behind The

Music, along with breakthrough programs including *Pop-Up Videos* and *Storytellers.* The new shows propelled VH1's ratings and legitimized the channel among music fans.

Chapter 10

JOE WALSH SHREDS
THE SHERATON

"They say I'm crazy, but I have a good time…
Life's been good to me, so far."

Joe Walsh "Life's Been Good"

By most accounts, the Eagles broke up right after their concert on July 31, 1980, in Long Beach, California. They were raking in millions of dollars. But most of the money went to the band's songwriters, Glenn Frey and Don Henley. Over time, guitarist Don Felder's resentment grew, and it boiled over onstage one night in California. Often called the "Long Night at Wrong Beach", the shit hit the fan and band members reportedly threatened to kick each others' asses during the concert.

The Eagles had ridden a tidal wave of success and needed time to cool off. So they took what turned out to be a ten-year hiatus, and the band members went their separate ways. Joe Walsh spent those years in studios, recording with artists including Ringo, the Who's John Entwistle, and Dan Fogelberg. He kept a low profile and released a few solo albums, with little fanfare. But Joe really ached to play with a band again. Secretly, Joe Walsh dreamed of the day when he would get the call to reunite with the Eagles. He was so desperate to perform that Walsh briefly joined an Australian group called the Party Boys.

In 1990, I heard that Joe wanted to be a disc jockey. Apparently he did a fill-in show for a station back East. My first thought was to hire Joe as a guest DJ for a whole week. Then I considered Joe's notorious reputation for drinking and partying out of control. I wondered, how would he sound on the air? In interviews, Walsh comes across like a stoner, à la Jeff Spicoli in *Fast Times at Ridgemont High.* "Hey dude, let's party!" Then again, Joe's a cool guy, a rock superstar, and a *perfect* fit for KISW's bad boy reputation. So, I called Walsh's manager, David Spero, to see if Joe would be interested in spending a week in Seattle.

I told Mr. Spero, "We'd like to invite Joe to be our morning DJ next month."

He asked, "When you say morning DJ, what hours would Joe be on-air?"

"I'm thinking from 6 a.m. to 10 a.m."

Spero laughed and said, "Forget it. Joe doesn't even wake up until noon!" Not to be denied, I quickly countered with, "What if we have Joe host the afternoon show from 2 p.m. til 6 p.m.?"

Spero considered my offer, and before he could shut me down again, I added, "We can pay him $10,000 for the week, plus Joe's airfare and hotel."

Walsh's manager paused for a minute to mull my offer, then replied, "That might work. Let me talk it over with Joe."

A few days passed and I got a call from Smokey Wendell. Officially, Smokey is Joe's tour manager. Unofficially, he keeps Joe on the rails. Smokey called to confirm that Joe Walsh wanted to host the afternoon slot, live from KISW's studios in Seattle. And after his final radio show on Friday, Joe would perform a free concert for our listeners.

"That's awesome, Smokey," I celebrated, pumping my fist in the air. "I'll send you the details."

Now, my biggest challenge was to get the blessing from my bosses at Nationwide Insurance in Columbus, Ohio. Not the hippest rock fans, the insurance men aim to avoid trouble at all costs. I was sure that Joe Walsh was way out of their comfort zone. This would surely test their slogan "Nationwide is on your side."

I scheduled a conference call and envisioned several corn-fed insurance men gathered around the speakerphone in Columbus. Pale, bland, Midwesterners whose musical tastes leaned more toward Frank Sinatra than Frank Zappa. I explained, "We've got a rare opportunity to have a bona fide rock star on our radio station. Just think of the new listeners we can draw!" I moved in for the close. "I'd like to hire Joe Walsh to be a DJ for one week. And I need your okay to pay him $10,000."

I heard crickets. Tumbleweeds blew by. I wondered, had they hung up? Were they scribbling on their notepads, "Fire this idiot"? One Nationwider spoke up with, "I think this is a good idea." I was stunned that the insurance execs had even heard of Walsh. But as it happens, Joe was from Cleveland, a preapproved member of the "I'm From Ohio" club.

After working out the contract language, performance clauses, and payment schedules, my bosses gave me the green light to hire Joe Walsh for one week. But they made it clear: "Nationwide likes collecting premiums, not paying claims. So, we will pay him the $10,000. But we know about Joe's reputation. So we're holding you responsible if there's any trouble."

Gulp. I assured Nationwide that everything would go smoothly. Little did I know.

Next, I needed hotel rooms for Joe Walsh and Smokey Wendell. The manager of the Seattle Sheraton was a friend. So I called her and explained that I wanted to book two nice hotel rooms next month, for Joe Walsh and Smokey Wendell.

"Is that *the* Joe Walsh? Joe Walsh from the Eagles?" she asked.

"Yes, *the* Joe Walsh."

"Wow," she exclaimed, "How exciting. We'd love to have him stay at the Sheraton. I'll give them both free rooms and upgrade them to our deluxe suites. But...." Then came the question that I'd hoped to avoid. She followed up with, "I've heard stories about Joe demolishing hotel rooms. Can you promise me that he will behave?"

Hmmm. Legend has it that Walsh once brought a chainsaw on tour with the Eagles and used it to cut holes in the walls between hotel rooms when the doors were locked. Voila! Adjoining rooms! I responded, "Of course. Joe will behave. He doesn't do that anymore." Or so I thought.

In October of 1991, Joe Walsh walked through the front door of KISW's lobby followed by his road manager. We shook hands, and I led them around the station, introducing Joe and Smokey to our staff. The KISW crew was charmed by Joe. He's got an easygoing style and is impossible not to like. To his credit, Walsh greeted everyone with a smile, looked them in the eye and (in his best Spicoli voice) asked, "How ya doin'?"—his signature line. Joe is a giant among rock guitarists. But there's no star attitude. He is very relaxed and humble. Nothing seemed to faze him.

After meeting our team, Joe, Smokey and I retreated to my office. I handed over the $10,000 check along with room keys for the Sheraton. Then, we discussed some details about his radio show. While most radio personalities follow a fairly tight script, I sensed that Joe needed more latitude. So, I said, "Joe, I don't want to box you in with too many rules. So, just be yourself. Play great rock songs, talk to listeners on the phone, and have fun."

That was music to Joe's ears. He really wanted to do a good job and eagerly listened to what I had to say. Or so I thought.

The next day, I led Joe into our on-air studio and he took a seat behind the control board. The staff excitedly pressed their noses against the studio windows to watch a rock star in action. It was time to turn Joe Walsh loose on Seattle. At 2 p.m. sharp, he flipped on the microphone and said (not surprisingly), "How ya doin'?" So far, so good.

I called the Nationwide execs and proclaimed that Joe Walsh was live on KISW and that all ears were on him. They seemed moderately impressed, and couldn't wait to hang up and dive back into their spreadsheets.

Joe had been on the air for a short while when our music director buzzed me on the intercom. He asked "Do you recognize this song that Joe is playing?" I turned up the radio in my office and had no clue what the song was. We'd agreed that Joe would stick reasonably close to KISW's playlist. But he was already going rogue. So, I strolled down the hallway toward the studio and opened the control room door. "Hey Joe, how's it going so far?"

"Great, how ya doin'? Does my show sound good?"

I said "Yeah, we love having you here, Joe. By the way, what is this song called?"

Joe replied, "Uh, it's the Michael Stanley Band. They're from my hometown, Cleveland."

Not wanting to squash his spirit I said, "Okay. But after this song, let's get back to our playlist."

Joe assured me, "Sure, no problem."

An hour later, my phone buzzed, again. It was our music director again, sounding nervous, "Uh, Joe is playing 'Bang A Gong.' It's a cool song, but I've never heard this version. It sounds like there's extra guitars playing or something."

I turned up my radio and heard what he meant. It was the classic T. Rex tune, but somehow it did sound different. Back down the hallway, I pushed open the studio door. There, in the center of the room stood Joe Walsh, wailing away on his guitar. He had figured out how to plug his gold Les Paul into our control board and was playing guitar along with T. Rex's Marc Bolan. The speakers blasted "Bang A Gong" at full volume, while Walsh added lead guitar solos.

My first reaction was, "What the hell is he doing?" My second thought was, "How cool is that?" This was the crazy side of Joe, the spontaneous side that makes him so special. He broke all the rules, and our listeners were going nuts for him. Right then, I dismissed any concerns, thinking, "Nationwide and the Sheraton have nothing to worry about. Joe Walsh is a sweetheart. This week is going to be a piece of cake."

For a guy who wakes up at the crack of noon, I was impressed that Walsh showed up on time every day, raring to go. I had Smokey to thank for keeping him on schedule. I also relied on Smokey to keep Joe out of trouble, which is a mighty task considering his history. Smokey shadowed Walsh closely. But once Joe was in his hotel room, all bets were off. No one could babysit Joe 24/7. And that's where the trouble began.

While Joe Walsh was on the radio, Smokey hung out in my office. He is a very patient man with a calming presence.

He told me stories of trying to keep John Belushi out of trouble. Turns out, that was too much responsibility for anyone. Smokey tried to help straighten him out but finally told the SNL legend that it was time to be responsible for his own life. Weeks later, Smokey was crushed to learn that Belushi had died. But he wasn't surprised. He also confided that Joe Walsh was a challenge and was still drinking heavily. But Smokey was there to rein him in. As much as anyone could.

As a frame of reference, Wendell's previous client was John Belushi. He was John's constant companion, but stopped working with Belushi just weeks before his death. Clearly, this man was battle-tested. Now, Smokey Wendell was Joe Walsh's wingman and would be traveling with him to Seattle. Smokey was *my* insurance policy!

On Thursday of that week, Joe and I were chatting in my office about thirty minutes before his Guest DJ show. We were interrupted when the receptionist knocked on my door and poked her head in. "Joe has an urgent call on line one." Walsh picked up the phone in my office and put the caller on the speaker.

"Joe, it's Irving." (as in Irving Azoff, the Eagles' manager).

"How ya doin', Irving?"

"Fine, Joe. Got a minute? I've got big news. The Eagles are getting back together."

Joe sat down, stunned by the news. His eyes were glazed and a grin crept across his face. He'd been waiting for this call for years. Azoff continued, "Don and Glenn want to tour next year and record a new album. Are you in?"

Joe grabbed the receiver and shouted, "Hell yes! I'm in! Look, I'm about to go on the radio now. Can I call you back tonight?"

Joe Walsh was ecstatic. "Henley and Frey said they'd only play together again when they ran out of money, or if hell freezes over. They're both loaded. So it must be a cold day in hell."

I felt happy for Joe, and privileged to hear the advance word that the long Eagles drought would soon be over. Walsh bounded down the hallway and headed for our studio control room. Today he'd host Double Shot Thursday, when KISW played two songs back-to-back by the same artist.

Joe started his show by playing two songs from Led Zeppelin followed by two from Aerosmith. We were off to a great start. So I turned down the radio and got back to work. Ten minutes later, the phone rang in my office. "How ya doin'? It's Joe. Hey, I got a question. There are two bands that drive me crazy. All of their songs sound the same to me. So, when I play those artists, can I get it over with and play their songs simultaneously?"

"Let me see if I understand." I clarified, "You want to play *both* songs at the same time?"

"Yeah," said Walsh. "It will go by faster if I play both songs together."

It was hard to argue with that logic. So, as I walked back to the studio, I tried to imagine how awful that would sound. I opened the door and asked, "Joe, who are the two artists that you want to play simultaneously?"

"Steve Miller and Phil Collins. Their songs all sound alike. I can't tell them apart. Do you think listeners will notice if I play two songs at once?"

I knew this was a bad idea. But in the spirit of compromise, I said, "Okay. Let's try it."

So Joe cued up Steve Miller's "Rock'n Me" and "Jet Airliner." He went on the air and explained his logic to our radio listeners and pressed play. At first, it was funny. I had to admit that the songs did sound similar. But even Joe had to agree that the Miller mishmash was too bizarre. With order restored, for the moment, I walked back down the hall to my office.

After Joe Walsh's Friday radio show, I drove Joe to a club on Seattle's north side. We capped the week with a private concert starring Joe Walsh. When he performs with the Eagles, Joe plays in large arenas and stadiums. On this night, about 500 listeners were treated to an intimate set from one of America's greatest rock guitarists. And it was magical. He was in rare form and treated the crowd to his biggest hits. Joe whipped out his talk box for "Rocky Mountain Way" and "Those Shoes." He wailed on "Funk #49" and slapped hands with fans between verses of "Life's Been Good." Decked out head to toe in KISW garb, Joe was worth every dime of our $10,000 investment.

After the concert, Joe, Smokey and I hugged and said our goodbyes. But the story doesn't end here. The following Monday, I got a call from my friend at the Sheraton. She asked, "Beau, who is going to pay Joe Walsh's hotel bill?"

"What bill?" I asked. "You told me that the rooms were free!"

"Yes, the rooms were free," she said. "But who's paying for his incidentals?"

I asked, "How much were his incidentals?"

She replied, "Joe Walsh rang up a $10,000 tab."

"What?? How can that be?"

My friend confided, "Well, about $1,500 was for liquor that Joe had delivered to his room."

Incredulous, I tried to clarify. "Joe drank $1,500 worth of booze in just five days?"

"Apparently. But wait until you hear about the other $8,500. From what we can tell, Joe shredded every piece of cloth in the room. If it could be ripped up, Mr. Walsh ripped it to shreds. It looks like he cut everything into long strips: sheets, blankets, towels and curtains. Everything. Our housekeepers walked into his room this morning and found a giant pile of fabric piled in the middle of the room."

I gulped as Ms. Sheraton added, "Our manager is freaking out and he wants this bill paid, today."

"Uhhh, I am so sorry," was the best I could muster. I wondered if Nationwide would be on my side (or my back) for this calamity.

My next call was to Smokey. He and Joe had returned to L.A. So I tracked him down and explained the situation with the Sheraton. Smokey patiently listened. After a few moments of silence, Wendell responded in his relaxed style, "Send me the hotel bill. I'll take care of it."

"Wow, just like that? We paid Joe ten grand to come here for a week. And he blew it all at the Sheraton?"

"Welcome to my life," he deadpanned.

The following year, Joe Walsh's prediction came true. The Eagles released an album called *Hell Freezes Over*.

So, how is Joe doin'? He has reportedly quit drinking and you can still catch him on tour with the Eagles. Yes, life's been good to him, so far.

After his week as a DJ, Joe Walsh capped it off with a private concert

....and got some love from his fans

Chapter 11

PAUL McCARTNEY AND
THE GIRL IN THE BLACK BERET

"And, in the end, the love you take,
is equal to the love you make."

The Beatles "The End"

Kelley was a nineteen-year-old who was suffering from brain cancer. She'd endured rounds of treatment, but the disease continued to spread. When doctors run out of options, they often call the Make-A-Wish Foundation and ask them to step in. When they asked Kelley, "What would you like more than anything in the world?" she responded, "My dream is to meet Paul McCartney."

While most sick children request a trip to Disney World, this request would be much harder to grant. Paul McCartney was the biggest rock star in the world. When Make-A-Wish called me to ask if I'd help fulfill Kelley's request, I told them I'd try. But this was a real long shot. I inquired, "Does Kelley have a Plan B?"

"No," they replied. "This is all that she wants."

I must admit that I was skeptical that a teenager was truly a Beatles fan. If I was going to lobby McCartney's "people," I needed to hear it for myself. That evening, I called Kelley's home and spoke with her and her mom. On the phone, Kelley was soft-spoken, shy and remarkably poised for a woman who'd been diagnosed with a terminal illness. I asked her when she first heard Paul's music.

"My mom was a child of the '60s and '70s, and I grew up listening to the Beatles and Wings. I know those albums by heart."

"Let's play a game, Kelley," I suggested. "Imagine that I have a machine that can print concert tickets for any artist. Who would you choose?"

"My friends think I'm crazy," Kelley admitted. "But I'm a huge Paul McCartney fan. I just love his songs and even have a stuffed Paul doll on my bed." Kelley convinced me that she was sincere. We spoke for another ten minutes before Kelly had to leave. This gave me a few moments to chat privately with her mother. "I will do everything I can to give Kelley a special experience," I assured her. "In your opinion, is this really what she wants?"

Without missing a beat, Kelley's mom answered, "Nothing would mean more to her than meeting Paul McCartney."

"Okay. Let me go to work. A lot of people must sign off on this request before it gets to Paul. I'll make some calls and keep you posted." While I really wanted to make this happen for Kelley, I knew that her chances were slim and none. Still, it was hard to manage their expectations.

As luck would have it, McCartney's tour was passing through Seattle the following month, March of 1990. This would be his first show in America since John Lennon was murdered on the streets of New York City. I had heard that Paul was keeping a very low profile and preferred to stay well under the radar. I didn't want to disappoint Kelley. But getting a private meeting with Paul would be a real challenge. I sent letters to McCartney's manager and followed up with phone calls. I explained that Kelley had only months to live and her final wish was to meet Paul McCartney. I poured it on, "It would mean the world to her if Paul could spare a few moments." I went back to McCartney's record label and begged his PR agency. But no luck. The answer was the same. "Sorry, but Paul has asked for privacy and is not meeting people on this trip."

I called Kelley and told her that I had played every card that I could, but the chances of meeting Paul were looking grim. Kelley and her mom took the news graciously and thanked me for trying.

Never one to accept defeat, I took one last shot and begged McCartney's management again. I appealed to Paul as a father of a nineteen-year-old daughter (Stella) and hoped that he'd sympathize with Kelley's plight. A few days later, I got the call that I was hoping for. A rep from McCartney's firm, MPL Communications said, "Paul has agreed to see Kelley at 3 p.m. on the day of his Seattle concert, right before his sound check."

I was bursting inside. His rep went on to say, "We will arrange for three backstage passes for you, Kelley and her mother."

"That's perfect," I gushed. "Thank you so much."

"However," his agent said, "Paul has one stipulation. Nobody can know that he's doing this. He doesn't want any press people there when he meets Kelley. Mr. McCartney wants this to be a private meeting, as it should be. No reporters can be present. He's meeting Kelley because he cares, as the father of a teenage girl."

I excitedly called Kelley and her mom and gave them the good news. "You're not going to believe this, but Paul McCartney said yes! He will meet Kelley on March 29th before he goes on stage." They squealed with delight.

My plea clearly struck a chord. McCartney had a reputation as a family man who made his four daughters and son a priority. Kelley's terminal illness must have resonated with him, and Paul was making a special effort to see her. Make-A-Wish and I agreed to tell no one until after Kelley's private meeting with her idol. We all agreed that the man showed tremendous class by agreeing to see her, for all of the right reasons.

On the afternoon of McCartney's sold-out concert, I rendezvoused with Kelley and her mother at the backstage entrance to the Kingdome. We had never met in person, only spoken by phone. So I was anxious to get to know this young, strong-willed Beatles fan. Kelley stood about five feet tall, and she was rail thin. She was soft-spoken and shy, but her smile was infectious. Kelley had lost all of her hair after exhaustive radiation treatments, but still looked terrific in a black beret. She beamed, "My mom took me clothes shopping, and I picked out this patterned dress and beret. I hope Paul likes it."

"You look adorable, Kelley," I said. "Let's go meet Paul McCartney." With that, she clutched her stuffed Paul doll under her arm along with several photos and album covers for him to sign. I escorted Kelley and her mom inside the concrete and steel dome, and they were overwhelmed by the enormity of the empty stadium. The floor was lined with thousands of empty folding chairs, filling what was usually the Seahawks' playing field. We dodged the crews who were setting up Paul's equipment onstage, hanging lighting trusses and preparing for his sound check. In just a few hours, this cavernous dome would be packed with 50,000 screaming McCartney fans. But for now, we would have Paul and the Kingdome to ourselves.

The three of us were guided through several corridors to the backstage area and led to a twenty- by twenty-foot greenroom. It was sectioned off with aluminum pipes, long, red drapes and ugly green astroturf. Not very quaint, but it didn't matter. This moment was all about Kelley getting her wish. We sat in folding chairs in the center of the room, our hearts racing. Kelley nervously asked, "I know that Paul is an advocate for world peace. So I made him a peace pin. Is it okay if I give it to him?"

"Of course," I replied. "I'm sure he'll love it."

Moments later, the curtain parted and Paul's smiling face peeked out. He looked our way and smiled, "Are you Kelley?"

Stunned, Kelley turned to face Paul and meekly replied, "Yes."

My heart leapt when Paul McCartney pulled back the curtain and walked right

I've met many stars at backstage "meet and greets." Usually, you're rushed through a receiving line and only have time to say a quick hello and get a handshake before being ushered away. I was hoping that Paul would spend a few quality minutes with Kelley.

over to Kelley. She stood up and put out her hand. Instead of shaking it, Paul threw his arms around her and hugged her tightly. Then he and his wife Linda sat down on either side of Kelley and made her the center of attention. Her mother and I looked on as the McCartneys focused all of their attention on Kelley.

At one point, Paul took Kelley's hand and complimented her, "I love your beret. Do you think I'd look good in one?" Then he picked up the stuffed likeness of him that Kelley had brought. Paul held the doll next to his face and playfully remarked, "Which Beatle is this?" He made Kelley laugh when he joked, "Does it look like me? I thought I was supposed to be the cute Beatle."

Taking her cue, Linda reached into her bag and handed Kelley a stuffed bear they had brought for her. "Here Kelley, this is for you," said Linda. For a few precious minutes, the frail young woman forgot that she was fighting brain cancer. She savored this moment, closed her eyes tightly and pulled the stuffed bear to her chest. I looked over at Kelley's mom and saw that tears were streaming down her face. The sight of her daughter realizing her greatest dream was overwhelming. I felt a lump in my throat as I watched Paul and Linda, who were thoroughly engrossed. They could not have been more sincere and genuine. For now, Paul McCartney was not a rock star, he was a caring dad lifting the spirits of a young girl.

After about thirty minutes, Paul asked, "Kelley, what is your favorite Beatles song?" She responded "'The End.' I love where you sing, 'The love you take is equal to the love you make."

"It's really true, isn't it?" Paul added, "I've spent years talking about peace on earth, love and understanding. Do you believe in peace, Kelley?"

"I do. In fact, I brought something for you." Kelley reached into her purse and pulled out the pin she'd made in the shape of a peace sign and handed it to Paul. He turned it over in his hands and pinned it to his jacket lapel. "Darlin'," he said. "I'm wearing this onstage tonight."

With that, Paul stood up and reached out his hand to Kelley and winked, "Now follow me."

Paul led us back out into the arena and headed for the merchandise tables. They were piled high with McCartney shirts, jackets, sweatshirts, caps and posters. In a few hours, the crowd would make a dent in those piles and spend thousands of dollars on concert gear.

Paul turned to Kelley as she took in all of the cool McCartney swag. Then he asked, "What would you like?"

"Uhhh, can I have a shirt please?" Kelley replied.

Paul smiled, "I think we can do better than that, luv. Here, put out your arms." He proceeded to lift stacks of clothing from the tables and drape them over Kelley's outstretched arms. Literally dozens of items. Kelly thanked Paul profusely, as she handed the pile of clothing to her mother.

"We're not finished," Paul said. He took Kelley's arm and led us toward the stage and seated the three of us in the front row. Then he jumped on stage to rehearse a few songs while Kelley watched in awe. We were the only people in the Kingdome—and she was getting a private concert from Paul McCartney! He played "Hey Jude" and "Band On The Run," and he winked impishly at Kelley throughout his sound check. When he played the Beatles' classic "Get Back," Paul changed the character's name (Jojo) and sang "Get back, Kelley." She was swooning, her eyes sparkling.

After the rehearsal, Paul jumped down from the stage and walked straight toward Kelley. "I've got to go now and rest up before the show. Do you have concert tickets for tonight?"

"No," Kelley replied. "We tried to buy some but they were all sold out."

"Well, I can fix that. Tonight, you are my guest," McCartney said as he reached into his pocket and handed Kelley a pair of "all access" passes. "You've got the best seats in the house. We'll put special seats on the sound mixing board in the center of the arena." Kelley was stunned by his kindness and at last the tears started flowing. After a few more hugs and pictures, Paul disappeared into the caverns of the Kingdome—and we headed back to reality. It was a mind-boggling experience for me, much less a teen cancer patient. An hour after entering the Kingdome we were back in the parking lot wondering, "did that really happen?"

Two weeks later, I received a FedEx package with an autographed photo, signed from Paul to Kelley. I am told that he insisted on writing a message to Kelley. It read, "To our Kelley, lots of love, babe!"

Six months later, I received the phone call that I'd been dreading. Kelley's mom called to say that Kelley had passed away peacefully. "You should know that meeting Paul McCartney was the highlight of Kelley's life. She cherished that day and never let go of the stuffed bear that he gave her."

I hung up the phone and felt the cold slap of reality. It didn't seem fair that a brave young woman only lived to nineteen. She never got to experience adult life or have children of her own. But she did experience something special...the humanity and humility of Paul McCartney. And for that brief moment, Kelley's dream came true.

Paul McCartney wearing the peace sign lapel pin
that Kelley made for him

Chapter 12

GRAND SLAM
SUMMER JAM

> "One good concert justifies a week of
> satisfaction at home."
>
> **Robert Plant**

The Grand Slam Summer Jam of 1983 took mega-concerts to the next level, offering four bands for the price of one. It was a package deal including Foreigner, Loverboy, Blue Öyster Cult, and Joan Jett. The artists traveled together and rocked stadiums across America, playing to 50,000-plus fans per night. As rock tours increased in popularity, fans outgrew the typical 15,000-seat concert halls. Those venues were great for the circus and boat shows. But superstar rock shows were made for stadiums.

All four bands were red hot at the time, with million-selling albums under their belts. Each group could sell a ton of concert tickets on its own. But when bundled together, the bands created a six-hour rock extravaganza that transformed enormo-dome venues around the country.

When the Grand Slam Summer Jam (GSSJ) was announced, KISW was itching to get heavily involved in promoting it. We wanted to be the "go to" rock station for fans. So, I was disappointed when the GSSJ concert promoter called to inform us that KZOK-FM, our competitor, would be the show's title sponsor. My disappointment turned to anger when he said, "I'm loading all of my ad budget on their station and don't need your help." He wanted to make it clear that, "Your station cannot be involved with the Grand Slam Summer Jam show, or the artists, in any way." I felt insulted to be brushed aside and silenced. KISW was the most popular rock station in town and had been an active supporter of the GSSJ bands. We played the hell out of their albums. But for some reason, the concert promoter froze us out.

This blatant slap in the face made us want to sponsor the show even more. So we plotted our revenge and drafted a letter to the man behind the Grand Slam Summer Jam. "As you requested, KISW will not be involved in your concert. In fact, we won't even acknowledge it or mention the show on-air. Furthermore, you may not buy any commercials on our station to promote it. As far as our listeners are concerned, there is no Grand Slam Summer Jam."

The four-band extravaganza was about three weeks away, to be held in Seattle's Kingdome. We called our Ticketmaster contact and asked how tickets were selling. He told us what we'd hoped to hear: "After an initial burst of sales, ticket sales for the Grand Slam Summer Jam have really stalled. They've sold about 18,000 so far." That number of people would fill one-third of the cavernous Kingdome. The promoter bet on the wrong horse and was about to lose his ass. He needed to sell at least 40,000 tickets just to break even. The Not-So-Grand Slam show was shaping up like a foul ball. Screw 'em.

We wondered how long it would take for the promoter to suck up his pride and call us. With ten days to go before the big show, ticket sales inched up to 19,000—then flatlined. When the promoter finally did call us, all of his bluster was gone. He sounded frazzled when he called to ask for a meeting "right away." He was desperate now, and the tables had turned. Now we held all the cards.

When the promoter arrived for our meeting, he could barely look us in the eye. We knew that he was facing financial disaster if ticket sales didn't pick up. We expected him to apologize and discuss how KISW might get involved. And that's exactly what happened. The promoter opened with, "Look, I was wrong. I am sorry for shutting your station out of the show. I know that I can't pull off this show without your help. I stand to lose a ton of money as it stands." We could sense the promoter's desperation when he closed with, "Is there *anything* we can do?"

Our station manager asked, "What do you have in mind?"

"For starters," he said, "I am now proposing that the Grand Slam Summer Jam be a neutral show with neither station as sponsor."

When he called for an urgent meeting, we knew it would come to this. The promoter had been insulting and arrogant. Now we applied the pressure and stated our terms. "Sure, we will help promote your Grand Slam Summer Jam. But we're not interested in being completely neutral. KISW needs to have some ownership of the concert." We were prepared to throw the kitchen sink at this concert and steal it from KZOK, with or without the promoter's blessing.

Our manager was salivating over the chance to make some money and continued, "First, you need to spend $40,000 to buy ads on our station. We'll help promote the Grand Slam Summer Jam, but it's going to cost you."

"Okay," said the promoter, "I expected that."

Our manager smiled and sat back as I added, "Also, we know that Foreigner, Loverboy, Joan Jett and Blue Öyster Cult will arrive in town the evening before the Kingdome show. So, we want to host a softball game with the members of all four bands."

"That's fine with me," the promoter agreed. "But you'll have to ask the bands yourself. I don't control their schedules."

"Of course," I nodded.

We applied the final squeeze and demanded, "But most importantly, we don't want KZOK to have *any* presence inside the Kingdome. None." I implied that we wanted this to be a neutral show, meaning neither station would be the title sponsor. "Let's keep it neutral" I said. "They are our direct competitor. So, I don't want to see their banners inside the venue—and they can't have their DJ onstage to introduce the bands."

What the promoter didn't know is that I'd already sent invitations to the four band managers and recruited their record labels to help us pull off a huge, exclusive, pre-concert event. We were poised to turn on our promotional jets.

"Done. No problem," the promoter quickly agreed. He promised that KZOK wouldn't be given any advantages.

What he didn't realize is that we intended to dominate this event and leave our competitor holding the bag. Let KZOK play by the rules. We smiled in agreement, shook hands with the promoter, and prepared to put our plan into motion.

Our jocks immediately started talking up the Grand Slam Summer Jam. We created on-air promos featuring the voices of the four headliners that teased a special event. Meanwhile, our promotion team booked the finest softball field in the city, complete with stadium seating, dugouts and concession stands.

Now it was my turn. I cracked open my Rolodex and called the four band managers. In keeping with the Grand Slam baseball theme, we thought it would be fun to pit our team of DJs against an all-star team of rock bands. I told the band managers about our pre-concert softball game and invited their groups to play softball against KISW's "Flys." As I laid out the plan for each manager, their responses were priceless.

Foreigner was the headlining act, riding high with hit songs like "Urgent" and "Juke Box Hero." They were also the first band to commit to playing against our DJs, though Foreigner's manager confessed, "Our guys are British. They've never even played softball."

"No problem," I said, "Tell them it's like playing cricket. It will be a loose, friendly game. Think of it as a chance for fans to see their favorite band up close." Foreigner's manager replied, "Okay, they will play. But don't embarrass them." Foreigner was in.

Loverboy had come out of nowhere with a huge debut album. The Vancouver band was immensely popular in nearby Seattle. Singer Mike Reno and Loverboy had released one of the fastest-selling debut albums in Columbia Records' history, fueled by the monster hits "Turn Me Loose" and "The Kid Is Hot Tonight." So, we really wanted them for our softball game. But Loverboy's manager had a similar concern. "Our guys are Canadian. They grew up on ice skates, not a softball field. I doubt they even know how to play. How about a hockey game instead?"

"It's summer," I countered. "In America, we play softball in the summer. 'Grand slam' is a baseball term, not a hockey term. C'mon, it'll be fun for the band to play softball and meet their fans." After some more wrangling, Loverboy was in.

Rock fans were eager to see the tough chick singer who belted out "I Love Rock 'n' Roll." Joan Jett was the only woman on the Grand Slam bill, but she was the easiest to recruit for our softball game. Her manager called right back and said, "Joan grew up with baseball. She's a Baltimore Orioles fan and a pretty good athlete. She really wants to play, but she has to play second base."

God knows why that's important. I assured him "that won't be a problem" and added Joan Jett to the All-Star player roster.

Finally, I turned my attention to Blue Öyster Cult, the boys behind the classic "Don't Fear The Reaper." BÖC grew up on Long Island, New York. Surely these all-American boys could play softball. "Our guys aren't much into sports," said their manager. "They have zero baseball skills and were probably the last guys to get chosen in schoolyard games. But if all of the other bands are coming, at least one of the guys will play in your game." Done.

All four bands were confirmed to play in our softball game. When we announced our Grand Slam *Baseball* Jam on-air, KZOK was stunned. We were stealing the show from right under them, and we didn't stop there. Our DJs pumped the "Battle in Seattle" on-air, and the bands called in from the road to promote their show. The day before the concert, Foreigner, Loverboy, Joan and BÖC all came to our studios and played guest DJ.

Ticket sales started jumping: 25,000...30,000...35,000 and rising.

This would be Seattle's biggest concert of the year. To get all four bands to appear at our softball game was unprecedented. So we did it up right and created personalized jerseys for each of our celebrity players and ordered limos so they could travel in style. We alerted the press and created a special section where they could interview the stars. At the softball field, we set up speakers in the outfield and blasted our radio station during the game.

Joan Jett was the first to arrive at the softball field, decked out in a Columbus Knights baseball jersey and Baltimore Orioles cap. She brought her own glove and was ready for action. The rest of the Grand Slam team looked totally out of place. Mike Reno stepped out of his limo dressed for the Polo Lounge at the Beverly Hills Hotel. He was resplendent in a red and white headband, white linen sport coat, designer shades and super-short shorts. C'mon man, this is sandlot softball!

The Brits from Foreigner were totally bewildered, having never set foot on a softball field before. We had to give a quick primer on softball. Singer Lou Gramm had never worn a baseball glove or held a bat. Seeing the English bandmates try on baseball gloves was like watching cavemen discover fire. They had no clue.

One member from Blue Öyster Cult showed up, but opted to sit on the bench. Or "ride the pine" as they say in baseball lingo.

About 500 fans filled the seats behind home plate and stood along the foul lines. More were seated on blankets around the outfield. The players were literally surrounded by fans. The game started with player introductions and the crowd cheered wildly as their heroes stepped up to the plate. It didn't take long to realize that the rock all-stars were no match for our DJs. Not that our team was very good. The musicians were that dreadful. Granted, the guys in Foreigner and Loverboy hadn't a clue how to play baseball. And while Joan Jett was a stud at second, she was the only rocker with any skills.

Within twenty minutes, the friendly softball game turned into a drubbing. The rock all-stars were flailing, swinging wildly and missing almost every pitch. Loverboy's Mike Reno held his bat like a hockey stick, with similar results. Poor Lou

Gramm ran around the outfield in circles chasing fly balls. Joan Jett lived up to her billing and played hard, by far the best player on the all-stars' team. She was a good hitter, a deft fielder, and she had a strong throwing arm. But Joan's skills weren't enough to save her dreadful team.

We didn't want to humiliate the rock stars in front of their fans, so we lightened up and stopped keeping score. When one of their players reached base, we'd run out to hand them a beer. As the All-Stars came up to hit, our announcers poked fun. "Now batting, Paul Dean from Loverboy. His bio says that Paul plays guitar, raises gerbils, and owns Canada's largest collection of used gum." Of all the rock stars, Loverboy's singer Mike Reno made the girls squeal the loudest. The "man in the headband" played to the ladies in the crowd while flashing a toothy grin. Every so often, a girl would charge on the field and try to kiss him. Reno ate up the attention. But soon, more and more girls were chasing him down, sprinting onto the field from every angle. Our two security guys had their hands full, peeling young women off of Mr. Loverboy.

The drubbing lasted about ninety minutes. No matter how hard we tried to lose the game, the rock stars played even worse. So we decided to implement a mercy rule and end the game to avoid pissing them off. By now, the crowd had swelled to about 2,000 people as word got around that the Grand Slam Summer Jam bands were at the Woodland Park baseball field. It was great to let our listeners get so close to their heroes. But this crowd was spilling out onto the field and was too large for our security duo to control. I pulled Reno aside and said, "Mike, we're going to wrap up the game right after you hit. You'll be the last batter of the game."

He nodded "Okay, what do you want me to do?"

"You'll get mobbed if we just end the game now. So, we've got to be a bit sneaky and get the bands out of here safely. When it's your turn to bat, we will pitch the ball very slowly, making it easy for you. Swing hard and hit the ball. Then keep running around the bases. Our players won't try to throw you out. So, no matter where you hit the ball, just keep running until you cross home plate. Don't stop. Just keep running around the bases. Got it?"

Reno nodded again, solemnly. "Got it. Just keep running around the bases. Then what?"

I continued, "Your limo will be parked right behind the dugout. So, after you cross home plate, keep running straight into the car and close the door. Before anybody realizes what happened, you'll be gone."

Reno nodded, "Okay. Sounds like a plan."

Loverboy's singer was due to bat second that inning, and our team had been briefed on the plan. The limo rolled into place about twenty feet behind home plate, As Reno stepped up to the plate, he looked at me and nodded, acknowledging that he knew our team would fumble the ball while he circled the bases.

Reno mopped his brow with his famous headband and tossed it into the crowd. Women grabbed for the sweaty cloth as if it were a bridal bouquet. The mighty Reno strutted toward the plate and lifted bat to shoulder. We lobbed a fat pitch toward home plate and Mike swung with all of his might. He hit the ball off the end of the bat, just hard enough to send it dribbling slowly to the right side of the infield. Our player intentionally muffed the ground ball and threw it over our first baseman's head. While our fielders ran after the ball, Reno raced around first base and headed toward second. Then he stopped, dead in his tracks!

Reno was so proud of his feat that he completely forgot my instructions. He just stood frozen in the middle of the field with a shit-eatin' grin on his face. Meanwhile his fans were squealing with delight at Mike's stunning feat. Within moments, women were pouring out of the stands and onto the field to congratulate their hero. From the sidelines, I frantically waved my arms for Reno to keep running. Our players saw me flailing and started pushing Reno toward third. My jocks ran alongside him, acting like a human shield, to keep fans off of him.

Rounding third and heading for home, Reno waved to his adoring fans while I cleared a path from home plate to the waiting limousine. The driver saw Reno heading his way and opened the rear door. The king of Loverboy pranced toward the car, beaming like a Little Leaguer who'd just hit his first home run. He gave me a high five as he launched himself into the back seat. The driver slammed the door and jumped behind the wheel. The limo pulled away in a cloud of dust as throngs of women ran alongside the car, slowing its progress. The ladies were persistent and wanted a piece of Mike Reno's short shorts. Women were crawling all over the hood, valiantly straining to hang on. But one by one they gave up and fell away. I heaved a huge sigh of relief as Reno made his escape. Meanwhile, the remaining All-Stars sprinted for their limos and raced back to their hotel. In a few hours they'd all be taking the stage in the Grand Slam Summer Jam.

I cleaned up at the radio station before driving to the Kingdome. I got there an hour early and ran into the promoter inside the stadium. I looked up and pointed to a small KZOK banner hanging from the press box. I reminded him, "You promised that KZOK would not hang a banner tonight. But there it is."

The promoter blanched. "Sorry. But I don't have time to deal with this now. Do you have a station banner to hang next to theirs?"

"Yes," I answered with a sly grin.

"Then why don't you hang your banner, too?" Again, pointing to the upper level.

"Great suggestion, thank you. We'll hang ours next to theirs." I immediately agreed to his suggestion and instructed our promotion interns to haul our biggest banner up to the press box. Watching our sign unfold from down below was a sight to behold. As fans entered the Kingdome, they'd see KISW's forty-foot banner next to KZOK's eight footer. Booya!

Next, I located my morning DJs and walked with them toward the stage. "Guys, now we're going to rub it in KZOK's face." I reached into my pocket and gave them a $100 bill and said, "Do you see that guy onstage wearing the black ball cap? He's the stage manager and calls all of the shots. So go up to him, hand him the hundred and say, 'We are from the radio station and are here to introduce the bands.' "

The DJs looked at me like I was crazy. "You said that this was a neutral show and *nobody* is supposed to do stage announcements."

"That's true," I admitted, "But the stage manager doesn't know that. And I'll bet he understands a $100 bill. Trust me, just give him the cash and he will tell you what to do."

The two DJs made a beeline toward the man in the black cap. He was a large and heavily muscled man, standing about eighty feet away and barking out orders to the roadies. As my DJs approached the stage manager, he turned and shot them a stern look. I could see him mouth, "What the hell do you want?" My jocks, who acted like lions in the comfort of our studio, were reduced to lambs. Intimidated, they cowered and explained that they were the emcees for tonight's show. Then, one of my guys reached into his jacket, pulled out the $100 bill and handed it over. The dude in the black cap smiled as he snagged the bill and stuffed it into his jeans pocket. He pointed to the backstage curtain and directed my DJs to wait there for their cue.

At 4 p.m., the house lights dimmed and 51,000 fans roared with anticipation. A spotlight was aimed at the microphone in the center of the stage. On cue, the curtains parted and out walked my two jocks. They stepped up to the mic and welcomed the crowd on behalf of KISW (while the clowns at KZOK seethed). As our guys turned to leave, Joan Jett took the stage and slapped our jocks with a high five.

In the end, we thrilled the fans, clobbered the All-Stars, deflated KZOK and made the promoter rich. A Grand Slam indeed.

Joan Jett gives Loverboy's Mike Reno some baseball tips

Foreigner's singer Lou Gramm holds a bat for the first time

Joan Jett signs up a new fan

Chapter 13

GOLFING WITH
JIMI HENDRIX's DAD

"Aw shucks, if my daddy could see me now."

Jimi Hendrix "Up From the Skies"

There are two seasons in Seattle—winter and August. So, if you're a golfer, you get used to playing on soggy courses and stuffing your pant cuffs in your socks. One rare sunny day in 1986, I ducked out for a quick nine holes at Jefferson Park Golf Course. It's in the Beacon Hill section of Seattle, a middle-class neighborhood. I walked into the clubhouse and signed up as a single player, expecting to get paired up with three other duffers.

I walked over to the first hole as the golf course starter announced, "On the tee, Johnson twosome, Phillips single, and Hendricks single." As is customary, the four of us shook hands and teed off. The Johnsons drove away in a golf cart while Mr. Hendricks and I sauntered down the first fairway.

You can learn a lot about someone over five hours of golf. After eighteen holes, your true character is on display. It's fascinating to observe how golfers control their emotions and if they play an honest game. When I get paired with single players, I often sidle up to them and say hello. If nothing else, I can relate to a fellow hacker to who shares my pain. As Mr. Hendricks and I zigzagged down the fairways, I found myself staring at him. His face looked vaguely familiar, but I couldn't place him. I kept walking for another hole or two—and then it hit me. My golfing partner looked like a seventy-year-old version of Jimi Hendrix. Could he be Jimi's dad? I knew that Jimi grew up in Seattle and still had family in the Beacon Hill area. But Hendricks (or Hendrix) is a common surname. And Jimi's family was notoriously private.

I kept chasing my ball down the fairway, but couldn't stop thinking about the resemblance. As we walked toward the putting green, I drummed up the courage to ask, "Sir, may I ask your first name?"

He smiled and answered, "Hi, I'm Al. Al Hendrix," and reached out to shake hands.

"Nice to meet you," I replied as my brain whirred into overdrive. I was pretty sure that Jimi's father was named Al, but I'd never seen his picture. He sure looked like Jimi. Could this be *the* Al Hendrix, father of the world's greatest rock guitarist?

My golf partner was a soft-spoken black gentleman with an easy smile. I had to know. So I cautiously followed with, "By chance are you Al Hendrix, Jimi's father?"

Without missing a beat, he beamed, "Yes, I am."

On the outside, I remained calm. Inside, my heart was doing somersaults. "Are you kidding me? I'm playing golf with Jimi Hendrix's dad?!" I'd planned on playing just nine holes. But I would have played ninety holes if Al Hendrix was up for it. So, I paced myself. I'm sure that Al has been pestered about his famous son for years, probably decades. On this day, he had finally got a chance to relax and play golf—and he bumped into me. I didn't want to annoy Jimi's father. But I couldn't miss the opportunity to ask Al Hendrix about his son. So, I waited a few holes and left Al alone for a while as my mind raced. Then, our golf balls found the same pond and I started my not-so-subtle probing. "Do you mind if I ask you about Jimi? Does it bother you?"

"I don't mind. Not at all," Al smiled. "But I don't really have much to say. It was such a long time ago, and after he became famous I didn't see Jimi very often." Al was a gentle soul who didn't volunteer much. So, I was careful not to overplay my hand. After some light prodding, Mr. Hendrix revealed, "Jimi's real name was Johnny. When he was born, I named him Johnny Allen Hendrix. When he was about five years old, he came to me and said, 'I want to change my name and spell it J-I-M-I.' He was always unique, even as a child."

I was now so distracted that my golf game completely hit the skids. When I wasn't hunting for my ball in the woods, I stayed close to Mr. Hendrix and hoped that he'd open up about his son. "What was Jimi like as a kid?" I probed.

"Jimi loved to experiment, and he was always curious and trying new things. So I wasn't surprised when he picked up a guitar and started making crazy sounds. When I saw pictures of him with an Afro and wearing those wild-colored clothes I thought, 'that's my Jimi.'"

I wanted to ask Al what every Hendrix fan wants to know. "Tell me something that most people don't know about your son." As we walked around the back nine, Mr. Hendrix slowly revealed that he was a single parent for most of Jimi's life. "One day, I brought home an old ukulele that I'd found and gave it to my son. Jimi was a quiet kid who wasn't really into sports. But he loved to watch TV and plunk on that ukulele."

Jimi Hendrix started out playing a ukulele? I felt like a gold prospector who'd just discovered a nugget. Al seemed to enjoy talking about his late son, so I didn't interrupt. "When Jimi was around twelve or thirteen, I bought him an electric guitar. It wasn't much, but it was all I could afford. Jimi played it all the time and after awhile, he started a band with some friends. I figured that's fine if it keeps him off the streets. As a teenager, Jimi started showing some serious interest in guitar, and his band booked some local gigs. He was bored playing cover songs. So I encouraged Jimi to play original stuff and be different."

Jimi left Seattle when he was nineteen to join the Army. He visited his folks in Seattle while on leave, but Al didn't see his son very often. After that, Jimi Hendrix moved to England, where his career took off. He was embraced by England's rock royalty when the Beatles, the Who, Eric Clapton and Jeff Beck took a liking to him. Jimi was a rock comet who burned hot for four years before dying at age twenty-seven of a drug overdose.

Al was loosening up, so I gently nudged him again. "Al, what kind of relationship did you have with Jimi?"

Mr. Hendrix smiled wistfully and looked down at the grass. "Jimi would call me from England every so often. I remember in 1966 he called and said, 'Dad, I'm about to hit the big time.' And he did, indeed." Al stared off in the distance as if he was reliving that phone call.

I could tell that Al Hendrix was devastated after learning of Jimi's death, and the pain didn't end there. "Jimi would have been upset at the way our family fought over his estate. After he died, I turned over everything Jimi owned to the lawyers for safekeeping. But in the end, I never saw his things again. And I lost all the rights to Jimi's music. I was given some of his clothes and guitars, but didn't get much money. I felt cheated by my own family."

Turns out, Al had a lot to say.

I spent a memorable afternoon chasing a small white ball with Al Hendrix. Neither of us played well. But Al was easy to talk with, and he liked to laugh. At the end of our round I wanted to stay in touch. So, I suggested, "Al, I manage a rock radio station here in Seattle. Your son Jimi is a super-hero to our listeners. If I send a limo to pick you up Friday evening, will you come to our anniversary party and meet his fans?"

Al smiled and said, "Yes, I'd like that."

Al Hendrix, father of the legendary Jimi Hendrix, was a guest of honor at KISW's 15th Birthday Party and received an engraved crystal award to celebrate Jimi's legacy.

Chapter 14

THE PARTY TO END
ALL PARTIES

"Live the party. Love the party. Be the party."

Anonymous

As parties go, this bash will go down as one of the most outrageous in rock history. It achieved the Holy Trinity, featuring sex, drugs and rock & roll. In the summer of 1986, stars flew in from around the world, on their dime, to help celebrate KISW's 15th birthday.

We wanted to mark this occasion with a memorable event, but we had no idea that it would be legendary. Rather than pat ourselves on the back for turning fifteen, our station decided to honor the bands that helped us get to the top. We wanted this party to be an exclusive, star-studded, "I was there" experience that would be talked about for years. So, I cracked open my Rolodex and started reaching out to every artist, manager and record label exec I knew. I called in every favor, pulled every string, and worked every angle to attract rock stars. I told them, "Your band has been a great ally over the years. Now we want to return the favor. We have engraved a beautiful, crystal award and want to present it to the band, in person, at our birthday party."

We made it hard for bands to say no. In my pitch, I listed all of the other bands that had committed to appear, when in fact none had confirmed yet. Then I talked with record labels about booking a great band to play at our party. I started at the top of my wish list and invited the Fabulous Thunderbirds. Thankfully, they were available and agreed to be our house band for the night. Their song "Tuff Enuff" was the #1 hit in the country. Not a bad start.

Heart's Ann and Nancy Wilson were the first to accept our invitation. Then came RSVPs from our Canadian pal Bryan Adams and members of Loverboy from up the road in Vancouver. Now we're talking.

I felt the momentum build as more artists started confirming. Journey's manager called to say that singer Steve Perry, guitarist Neal Schon, and keyboard player Jonathan Cain would be joining us. Aerosmith and David Lee Roth were touring, but offered to send a video message to play at our party. And Al Hendrix agreed to accept an award on behalf of his son, Jimi. Game on.

Still, I hoped to land a really big star. So, I shot for the moon and put a call in to Jimmy Page's manager. He answered the phone, and I nervously told him about our birthday party. I explained how some of the biggest bands had already confirmed. Then, I summoned the courage to ask, "Would Jimmy Page come?" Before he could say no, I added, "Jimmy will already be in town for a concert (with his band, the Firm). Maybe he can stop by our party after his show? We can send a limo to pick him up at the Four Seasons and take him back later."

Silence. Then Page's manager burst out laughing. "Jimmy doesn't even go to his *own* parties. I've been to his home when Jimmy doesn't even come down from his bedroom to join his guests."

I pushed a bit harder, "Can you just ask him? Maybe Jimmy can drop by for a while? I'll have a limo waiting for him. Pleeeaaasse!"

A long sigh, then, "Okay," Page's manager said, "Send me info on your party and I'll ask Jimmy. But don't count on it. This is a real long shot."

The guest list for our party was shaping up nicely. Journey, Loverboy, Heart, Bryan Adams and music by the Fabulous Thunderbirds. Plus Jimi's dad. And in my dreams, Jimmy Page.

Next, I needed to find the right venue. Fans are used to seeing superstars onstage in large arenas. They never get to meet the bands up close. At this party, I hoped that rock stars would step down from their pedestals and rub shoulders with our listeners. Going to a private party with rock gods milling around was the Holy Grail to rock fans and no radio station had ever thrown a party like that before.

I met with the owner of a club called Parker's and explained my vision for the greatest rock party of all time. He was excited and agreed to host our bash. While some rock clubs make you feel like you're standing in a giant urinal with bar stools, Parker's had class. It was a showplace that often attracted national acts. The club held 700 people and felt intimate, with a dozen private booths surrounding the dance floor.

Our DJs promoted our 15th birthday party on-air as a once-in-a-lifetime event, an evening that our listeners would never forget. On this night, fans would walk around the club and mingle with their heroes. We hoped that with all of those rock stars in the house, some of them would hop on stage and jam together, if they felt the urge. Maybe Neal Schon would pick up a guitar. Maybe Ann Wilson would boogie with fans on the dance floor while Loverboy hung out with listeners at the bar. Our listeners might snap a photo with Al Hendrix or find themselves standing next to Bryan Adams in the men's room. For those lucky enough to score tickets, this would be a spectacular night.

When we announced the talent lineup, it was like pouring gasoline on the inferno. With so many stars coming to the club, we knew that rock fans would do anything to get into our birthday party. If we put tickets on sale to the public, they would sell out in minutes. So we kept all of the party tickets in-house and gave them away on-air. Listeners had to "win to get in." Everyone I knew came out of the woodwork with their hand out. Even my mailman hit me up for a ticket. Classified ads popped up in the *Seattle Times* saying, "I will pay any price for two tickets to KISW's party." We got requests from top-shelf clients and employees of competing radio stations. Even the mayor's wife claimed to be a listener and asked for a pair.

Here was the problem. Our station had 350,000 listeners, and only 350 pairs of tickets. As great as this party would be, we knew that many loyal listeners would be pissed off. So, I met with a local TV station to talk about filming the concert for a special. It was the only way to give rock fans a peek at what happened inside Parker's that night. The TV station agreed to film the festivities and air a one-hour special, featuring highlights from our birthday bash.

One week before the big party, I got a call from Ken Kinnear and John Bauer, Seattle's top concert promoters. They asked, "How would you like to have a hot, new comedian open your show?"

"Sure," I replied, "That sounds great. Who is the comic?"

"His name is Sam Kinison. You've probably never heard of him. But he's in a new movie called *Back To School* with Rodney Dangerfield. We've been listening to Kinison's new CD and he's hilarious—but kinda dirty."

I thought, "Kinda dirty? How can it be too dirty for a rock audience?" Rock *should* be edgy. So I told John and Ken, "Yes, please invite Sam Kinison to open our party. Meanwhile, please send a copy of Sam's CD so I can hear what he sounds like."

They said they would. But that CD never arrived—and I soon learned why they never sent it.

On the night of our party, I picked up the Fabulous Thunderbirds' Kim Wilson and Jimmie Vaughan (Stevie Ray's brother) at their hotel and drove them to Parker's. The club looked magnificent, decked out with hundreds of silver helium balloons suspended from the ceiling. We displayed a huge 15th-birthday cake and set up autograph tables for each band. Outside, our guests were lined up around the block dressed in their finery and clutching their tickets. As fans entered Parker's, they were handed a program and led to the tables where our rock star guests were seated. Sitting shoulder-to-shoulder were Steve Perry, Neal Schon and Jonathan Cain from Journey, Ann and Nancy Wilson from Heart, Bryan Adams, members of Loverboy and Al Hendrix. Our guests collected autographs and posed for pictures as they moved down the reception line.

Sam Kinison's brand of comedy was best described as manic. He frantically screamed at the top of his lungs. Nothing was sacred or off-limits. Sam famously lambasted the people of Ethiopia for living in the desert. He yelled, "You don't need food. You need luggage! This is sand! Nothing grows here! Get the hell outta there and move where the food is!"

I spotted KISW's owner Lester Smith and his wife. This was the first (and last) station event that he ever attended. So I led them to a special booth that I'd held for them, close to the stage. The rest of the other semicircular booths were reserved for the bands, so they could have some privacy while still being accessible to the fans.

Once everyone was inside Parker's, the TV cameras started their five-minute countdown and the crowd buzzed with anticipation. I headed backstage to meet Sam Kinison and make sure that he was ready to open the show. I wandered around until I finally found Sam huddled in a dark corner. I introduced myself and reached out to shake hands. He looked up at me, and I was startled by his appearance. I'm not sure what I expected, but as Kinison raised his head, I saw a short, stocky guy with no neck, hunched over like a troll. Sam was dressed all in black, with wild, kinky hair poking out from under his black beret. His eyes were wild, electric. He ignored my extended hand and nervously said, "I need a table."

I asked, "You're going on stage in a few minutes. Why do you need a table?"

Sam said, "Just find me a table."

There was very little room backstage at Parker's and no tables in sight. Kinison pointed to a small bench that was holding the twelve crystal awards that we were handing out to artists that night.

"How about that one?" he asked.

Rather than argue with him, we started removing the glass statues and placed them on the floor. Kinison wiped the table top with his sleeve. Thankfully, nobody else was watching as Sam reached into his coat pocket, pulled out an envelope and dumped a large pile of white powder on the table. I had never seen so much cocaine. When Kinison started laying out the lines of coke, they nearly covered the two-foot-square table. Now, I've witnessed rock decadence firsthand. Still, I couldn't believe what Sam did next. He rolled up a $20 bill, bent over the table and began snorting one line after another...until the table was empty! He must have ingested an ounce of blow within three minutes. Enough to stagger an elephant. There was no way to stop Kinison without creating a scene. Now he was wired to the gills, and I fully expected his heart to explode right then and there. Instead, Sam stood up, wiped his nose, smiled at me and said, "I'm ready. Let's go!"

I left the backstage area and returned to my seat, braced for what might happen next. The house lights dimmed as the spotlight hit our DJ onstage. "Welcome to KISW's 15th birthday party. Tonight, you're in for a special treat. We'll bring some of rock's greatest artists on stage and present them with crystal awards, and thank them for helping our station stay number one. Then, the Fabulous Thunderbirds will play. And if we're lucky, some of the other stars here tonight might join them onstage. So get your cameras ready."

I looked over and saw Kinison nervously fidgeting near the side of the stage, hidden from view behind a curtain. Our DJ continued, "But first, let me introduce Sam Kinison, a hot, new comic who will soon appear with Rodney Dangerfield in a new movie called *Back To School.*"

Sam Kinison bounded on stage and immediately polarized the crowd. Within thirty seconds, half of the crowd was howling with laughter, while the other half watched in horror. Sam wasted no time before making everyone uncomfortable. "None of you guys know how to eat pussy." That got everyone's attention, so he continued, "You just lap your tongue up and down, like you're painting a fence. I'll show you how to eat pussy," Kinison said, then stuck out his tongue and swirled it around.

Many guys laughed out loud, while their dates looked shocked and squirmed uncomfortably. Nobody expected

Sam to go there. I was trying to gauge the crowd's reaction, when I noticed some stirring at the front booth. KISW's owner and his wife abruptly stood up and were headed for the lobby. I chased them down near the exit doors and begged them to stay. "Mr. Smith, I apologize for Sam. Please stay, we've got some wonderful things planned." But the damage had been done. It took years to get my boss to a station event, and just one minute for Sam Kinison to chase him away. Despite my pleas, the Smiths walked out the front door, never to return. Better start sending out resumes tomorrow, I thought.

After ten excruciating minutes, Kinison left the stage. Soon, the party was back in high gear. Fans had never been so close to so many stars at once. The booths were packed with artists and fans. The guys from Journey were having beers at the bar. Bryan Adams was surrounded by starstruck women. Loverboy held court at their booth. Al Hendrix took pictures with his son's fans, and Ann Wilson rocked the dance floor. I glanced at the corner booth that was reserved for Jimmy Page. It was still empty, and my hopes were fading.

An hour into the show, my headset clicked on. I heard the excited voice of our promotion director, who was stationed at the back door. "You're never going to believe whose limo just arrived...Jimmy Page is here!" I excitedly gasped, "Bring him in through the kitchen, and I'll meet you there." Along the way, I grabbed two security cops and said, "Follow me."

We rushed into the kitchen as Jimmy Page and his date came through the back door. I awkwardly introduced myself and thanked him for coming. But I doubt that Jimmy ever saw or heard me. When he looked up, his eyes were vacant. Page seemed lethargic and unfocused. Clearly, he wasn't in any shape to go on stage, or even find his booth.

Still, I was thrilled to have Jimmy Page at our party, in *any* condition. Then I glanced at his date. We didn't check her ID, but she looked like she'd skipped algebra class to join us. We ushered Page and his date through the crowd and got them settled into a private booth. Word spread through the crowd that the great Jimmy Page was in the house.

I went backstage and pushed the table that Kinison used to the center of the stage. The crystal awards glistened as the spotlight shone on the table, which had traces of white powder still smeared across its surface. One at a time, our DJs brought the honored guests on stage and presented them with their glass trophies. Journey, Heart, Loverboy, and Bryan Adams accepted their cut crystal awards and said a few words to the crowd. Al Hendrix was overwhelmed by the huge ovation and sheepishly accepted in honor of his son. Aerosmith and David Lee Roth checked in from the road. They thanked us for their award and looked larger-than-life on the giant video screen.

As the road crew cleared the stage for the Fabulous Thunderbirds, I went over to Journey's booth and saw Steve Perry chatting up our promotions intern. I squeezed in beside him and asked, "Steve, the Thunderbirds are about to start. Do you want to hop on stage for a song or two?" He was clearly more interested in my intern than performing. So, I wasn't surprised when Perry begged off. "Sorry man, my voice is too tired to sing tonight. Do you mind if she and I leave now?"

"Uhhh, okay Steve," I said and headed back over to Page's booth on the off chance he might sing onstage. I sat down in Jimmy's booth and saw that he was down for the count. His eyes were still rolled back in his head. That night, Page was too dazed and confused to play. But he stayed until the end of the party.

The lights went down and our DJ introduced the house band for the evening. "Ladies and gentlemen, it's time for some Texas boogie. These guys have toured with Eric Clapton and the Rolling Stones. But tonight, they are here for your dancing pleasure. Please welcome, from Austin, Texas, the Fabulous Thunderbirds!" The band opened with their smash "Wrap It Up," which sent fans running to the dance floor. I could see our listeners alongside rock stars as the sea of bodies grooved to the beat of the T-Birds.

I took off the headset, opened a beer, and took it all in. Connecting superstars and their fans was an overpowering experience. Those who got a ticket were in heaven. The energy inside Parker's kicked up a few notches as the grand finale jam capped a magical evening. The TV cameras rolled as Bryan Adams and Loverboy jumped on stage, grabbed guitars, and launched into a medley of '60s rock songs. The dance floor was packed and throbbing to the beat. I sure wished that Jimmy Page could've joined in. But as it turned out, he was saving his energy for what we'll call the "after party."

The next morning, I got a call from the limo driver who returned Jimmy Page back to the Four Seasons Hotel. Still recovering from the adrenaline rush, the chauffeur related this classic rock & roll moment: "After the party, I drove around to the back door at Parker's and waited for Page. When he and his date came out, I opened the rear door of the limo and they climbed in. Once inside, I rolled up the privacy glass divider and drove them to his hotel."

It was a quiet thirty-minute ride to downtown Seattle, with no sounds coming from the back seat. Page's limo pulled into the circular driveway and parked right in front of the hotel entrance. The driver recalled, "It was a busy night with lots of people going in and out of the Four Seasons. I walked around to the back of the car to let Jimmy and his date out. As I opened the rear door, four legs tumbled out. I did a double take and saw Jimmy lying on top of his date, stretched across the back seat. When the limo door opened, they were engaged in the throes of passion and not about to stop. With their legs hanging outside of the car, I couldn't close the door without crushing their legs. So I held the door like an idiot as Jimmy Page humped his date, trousers bunched around his ankles and his shoes still on."

The red-faced driver dutifully held the door until Page finished his business, in full view of everyone in the hotel lobby. "For about five excruciating minutes, I stood there smiling to the passersby, as they looked on in disbelief. Finally, Jimmy slid out of the limo, satisfied. He hitched up his pants as his date pulled down her dress, and they strolled arm in arm through the front door of the Four Seasons."

Just another day in the life of a rock god.

The Fabulous Thunderbirds jamming with Bryan Adams and Paul Dean

Fans meet the stars at our birthday bash
(l-r) Journey's Steve Perry, Jonathan Cain

Loverboy's Paul Dean with Heart's Nancy Wilson

*The Fabulous Thunderbirds with Bryan Adams (center)
and Paul Dean (bottom)*

Journey's Steve Perry arrives

Chapter 15

PLAYING PEEKABOO
WITH BOB DYLAN

"See the man with the stage fright
Just standin' up there to give it all his might."

Bob Dylan "Stage Fright"

In July of 1986, Tony Scott was a rock radio DJ in Denver. His station was sponsoring the summer concert series at Red Rocks, a spectacular outdoor amphitheater nestled in the foothills of the Rockies. Tony's job was to introduce bands as they took the stage.

One of the most anticipated shows that summer was Tom Petty with special guest, Bob Dylan. They were fellow bandmates in the Traveling Wilburys who teamed up for a co-headlining tour. One night Petty would start the show, the next Dylan would be the opening act.

Scott was the emcee for the Petty/Dylan concert and showed up at Red Rocks an hour early. On this night, he would first introduce Tom Petty, then two hours later, he'd walk out to center stage and bring on Bob Dylan. Scott had met dozens of rock stars, but had never been introduced to the legendary Bob Dylan. He secretly hoped that this would be his night.

Tony was a concert veteran who was used to dealing with quirky artists, feisty promoters and belligerent stage managers. So he stayed out of everyone's way and wandered around the backstage area until it was time to introduce Petty. Tony recalls, "I was standing behind the curtain near the side of the stage, just staring out at the crowd. Petty's road crew was making its final adjustments, so I kept to myself. A security guy asked me to move, so I walked behind Petty's equipment and stood behind the stage. I looked down the corridor to my left that led to the bands' dressing rooms, knowing that Tom could appear at any moment. Nobody was coming. But out of the corner of my eye, I thought I saw a head peek out of a dressing room, then duck back when I looked that way. I figured that I'd imagined it. So, I shrugged it off and turned my attention back to the natural sandstone amphitheater."

After a minute or two, Scott glanced back at the hallway, and the same thing happened again. He recalls, "I'd swear that I saw a head dart back inside the same room. I'm thinking, 'This is too weird. Is someone playing games with me?' But the strangest thing was that I could swear that the head belonged to Bob Dylan. I wondered, 'Why would Bob Dylan peek out of the doorway and then dive for cover when I looked back?' " Scott adjusted his position, hoping to identify the mystery man. "This time, I angled my head to look at the audience, but my peripheral vision allowed me to also see the dressing room corridor. I thought this would let me catch a better look at whoever was playing peekaboo with me. Sure enough, I saw a brown, curly head poke out of the doorway and look my way. I quickly turned in that direction and got a good look this time. It was indeed Bob Dylan staring back at me, and then ducking away. I was close enough to tell that Dylan wasn't pleased to see me. My suspicions were confirmed when his dressing room door swung open and an enormous security goon headed my way. The guy was a monster, fully equipped with a walkie-talkie, earpiece and baton. Bob was walking slightly behind him and pointing my way. The security guard came right up to me, and I stared straight ahead into his neck.

" 'You're going to have to leave the backstage area,' he said. 'You're making Mr. Dylan nervous.' "

"Unbelievable! I'm making Bob Dylan nervous!" Scott marveled. This was getting crazy, he thought. As Tony tells it, "I'm an easygoing guy who's just here to make the stage announcements. Why would Bob Dylan give a crap about me?' I wondered if maybe he was once threatened by someone who looked like me. Was it my Hawaiian shirt? Or maybe Bob rolled a fatty in his dressing room and wasn't himself. I wanted to be respectful. But I didn't deserve to be kicked out."

Scott didn't want to piss off the bodyguard, or Bob Dylan. So, he explained, "Look, I'm from the radio station that's sponsoring this show. I'm here to welcome the crowd and introduce the acts this evening. If you could just explain that to Bob, maybe he'd calm down."

"No. I must ask you to leave the backstage area." The big dude wasn't budging. "Mr. Dylan wants you to leave, now."

"That's fine," Tony relented. "Tell Bob that I'll leave this hallway. But first, I have to make a stage announcement." Tony fully expected the guy to put him in a hammerlock and crack his ribs with the baton. Instead, Dylan's goon motioned Scott to a spot behind the curtain and told him to stand there until it was time to welcome the crowd. The time came for Scott to introduce Petty, and everything went fine. "After the Heartbreakers took the stage, I left the backstage area and watched Tom Petty's show from my seat. After his set, Petty's crew was breaking down his equipment. So, I headed backstage to do my final stage duty of the evening—introducing Bob Dylan."

Tony Scott was cowering near the backstage curtains when he saw the same goon approaching, this time with urgency. "As promised, I'd moved away from the dressing room. So, I couldn't imagine why he seemed pissed again. He stepped up right in my face and demanded, 'Mr. Dylan insists you introduce him from a hidden location. Not from the stage.' "

"Uhh, okay," Scott agreed. "This was getting stranger by the minute. Playing peekaboo was bizarre. But now Dylan felt I was unsafe to be around."

Suddenly, the stage lights went dark, and Bob Dylan was led to the microphone by a roadie holding a flashlight. Tony was on the far side of the stage standing in the darkness and holding a wireless microphone. Bob glanced around but couldn't see him shielded by the curtain. The stage manager signaled Scott's cue, and he spoke into the mic, "Ladies and Gentlemen, please welcome one of the most influential figures in music, the great Bob Dylan." Later in the show, Scott recalls, "Dylan and Petty took the stage together for their encore. I looked up at Bob from my tenth-row seat, wondering if he'd see me and have a public meltdown."

Bob Dylan had a reputation as a man of mystery, uncomfortable around people and at times, reclusive. He once withdrew from the public and, apart from a few select appearances, did not tour for almost eight years. Johnny Cash is quoted as saying, "I think Bob Dylan was scared or even a little embarrassed performing. He's a very shy person. I've seen him come offstage, upset. He said, 'I'll be the laughingstock of the business! My fans are gonna laugh in my face.'"

Chapter 16

RATT, CAUGHT WITH THEIR PANTS DOWN

"In the '80s if you were in a rock band, when you asked for a hummer, you got a hummer."

RATT's Stephen Pearcy

Over the years, I spent a fair amount of time backstage and witnessed some bizarre moments. Too often, I found myself in the wrong place at the wrong time. But record labels often added me to their guest lists and invited me to meet the bands. It was good PR for them to meet radio people and take a few pictures. And I enjoyed tipping a beer with the rock gods and rising stars.

Most fans, when they envision going backstage at a rock concert, imagine a Hugh Hefneresque fantasy world—a flesh feast with loud music, cold drinks, and hot women. And that's how it was in the 1980s. Just ask the guys in Def Leppard about the orgies underneath the stage *during* their concerts. One by one, band members would sneak down below for a quickie while their mates played onstage.

Where were cell phone cameras when we needed them?

The backstage scene is fairly tame now by comparison. Gone are the glory days of outlandish backstage parties, like those that Cameron Crowe chronicled in the movie *Almost*

Famous. Drugs and drunken parties were fairly common well into the '90s, and I'm sure that some of that wildness still exists. But not on the same grand scale. Concert venues are more businesslike now, and most everyone is on their best behavior.

If you peeked backstage today, you'd see long, concrete tunnels littered with staging gear and equipment cases. Along the hallways are dozens of dressing rooms, better described as cinder-block holding tanks, where bands sit on couches and nibble from deli trays. Unless you're a mega-star, being backstage is fairly civilized and uneventful.

Not so in 1984.

Groupies were plucked like low-hanging fruit. The same handful of available ladies would show up at concerts all over town, looking for singers and guitar players to con-quer. Because I went to a lot of shows, I recognized the usual crowd of groupies who hung out by the backstage door, hoping to score a backstage pass and more. There were two types of groupies. First there were the young, fresh-faced girls who were fans of that particular band. They were innocents who just wanted to meet the group. Before they knew it, these girls were in the tour bus with their clothes off…more notches in the band's belt. Then there were the hardened veterans. It didn't matter which band was playing, these women were out to nail some-body. I'd often see Roxy, Teresa and the aptly named B.J. at shows. We knew each other by name, and we'd say hello, but that's about it. They weren't interested in a guy like me, and vice versa.

Many superstar bands skipped backstage trysts and brought the party back to their hotel. But the young bands were too horny and couldn't wait. Success was new, fun and exciting. So they prowled for young women at the show and brought them into the dressing room for quick sex. Who needed a hotel room when they could get down and dirty right there?

Before RATT hit the big time, KISW snagged them on their way to stardom and booked them to play one of our Rising Star concerts. Three thousand tickets went on sale and immediately sold out. The band was so hot, we could have sold out the theater five times.

On the night of the show, I was milling around the small backstage area, waiting for my cue to welcome the crowd. I waved to the five guys in RATT as they passed me on their way to the stage. One of them yelled, "Come up to our room after the show."

"Okay, sounds great," I called back.

After RATT's ninety-minute set, the Atlantic Records rep suggested we head up to the band's dressing room, a few floors above the theater. "I'm sure the guys want to thank you for all of your station's support." So, the Atlantic rep grabbed his hired photographer, and the three of us headed upstairs to hang out. We walked up a few flights of stairs, then down a nar-

The band RATT rose to fame in 1984, fueled by their hit song "Round and Round." The combination of radio airplay and MTV exposure catapulted this San Diego band to the top. One of the great hair bands of their era, RATT went on to sell millions of albums and packed stadium shows with Ozzy Osbourne, Iron Maiden and Mötley Crüe. Eventually, RATT found their natural touring partner and joined forces for the ever-popular RATT / Poison tour.

row hallway. We came upon RATT's lair and saw this sign taped to the door.

The guy from Atlantic Records knocked on the door. No answer. Moments later, he knocked again, a bit harder. "I know that they're in here," he said. "Follow me." He twisted the doorknob, swung open the door, and we stepped inside.

Then we immediately wished we hadn't.

We got about three feet into RATT's dressing room and came to a sudden stop. Ten sets of eyeballs turned to us with a look of surprise. Clearly, our timing was bad. Really bad. Embarrassingly bad. But I wasn't shocked by what we saw. After all, this was the dressing room of a bad-ass rock band in the '80s. Still, it was startling to walk in on the band mid-blowjob.

The room was the size of a small bedroom, with a table in the center holding gray tubs filled with beer. There was a shelf running along the far wall, where the five members of RATT sat, side by side. Each had his pants around his ankles and a young woman kneeling in front of him. I suppose there are a million lines I could have used. But I couldn't think of a single one. At that moment, I wasn't feeling clever, and all I could do was smile at the groupies I recognized. I meekly waved, "Hi Roxy, hi Teresa, hi B.J." The women stopped what they were doing just long enough to nod and acknowledge our presence. Then, they resumed working on the members of RATT.

Quietly, the record rep, the photographer and I backed out of the room and tiptoed down the stairs. Sorry, but there are no photographs to share with this story. And there's not enough "brain bleach" in the world to erase that scene from my mind.

Chapter 17

SORRY, DICKEY BETTS,
WE DRANK ALL YOUR BEER

"He was a wise man who invented beer."

Plato

This was hands down the strangest job interview, ever.

I worked as a rock radio DJ for a few years. But I always aspired to be the station's program director, the one responsible for choosing the music and hiring the DJs. I felt that I was ready to take that next step, if I could only get someone to give me a chance. As it happened, a radio station in Seattle was looking for a program director. I had never done that job before, but believed I had the skills. So I applied. As a rule, program directors must first prove themselves in small markets. I didn't want to work in Bumfuck, Idaho, and hoped to land a better gig. So, I set my sights on Seattle and bugged the general manager (GM) of KISW until he agreed to see me. I was not even on his radar and had nothing to lose. I pitched him every idea I had. After several meetings with the GM, he assured me that I had very little chance of getting the job.

I sent a follow-up package, outlining how I'd improve his station's ratings. After ten days passed without any word, I saw my chances dim. Then one day, the general manager surprised me with a call and asked me to meet him. He was close to making a final decision.

"Of course," I agreed. "Should I come to your office?"

"I've got a better idea," he said. "Meet me tonight at the Paramount Theater. We'll watch the Dickey Betts concert and find time to talk there."

For the sake of reference, Dickey Betts is best known as the former singer-songwriter-guitarist for the Allman Brothers Band. He was unceremoniously booted out of the band under murky circumstances. A few years later, Betts resurfaced with his new band, called Great Southern. It had to be humbling, after performing at stadiums, to be downsized and playing small theater shows, like this one.

I was eager to impress the general manager and hoped he had good news. So, we met that night in front of the Paramount. It's a beautifully renovated theater with thick carpets, spacious balconies and sweeping staircases. We walked inside the theater and found our seats as the opening band was introduced. It was forgettable. The manager and I left our seats before the end of their set, and he urged, "Let's head backstage." Behind the velvet curtains was a small, cramped area, filled with equipment cases and with wires snaking around the floor. Roadies were breaking down the first band's drum kit while Great Southern's crew started setting up their gear. No matter where we stood, it seemed that we were in someone's way. There was clearly no place for us to chat. So the general manager suggested, "Follow me, we'll go downstairs. There's a greenroom under the stage where we can talk privately."

"A greenroom under the stage?" That sounded cool.

We walked downstairs and entered a drab room with a linoleum tile floor. Not quite the same treatment that Dickey Betts got with the Allman Brothers. It was well-worn and sparsely furnished with two old couches, some folding chairs and a long table. The fluorescent lights flickered overhead as we plopped down to talk. For the moment, nobody was using that room. But, we could have been kicked out at any minute. So, I seized the opportunity and started to make my pitch to the radio manager.

Before long, we heard shuffling boot heels overhead and figured that Dickey's band was taking the stage. Moments later, we heard the announcer shouting from above, "Ladies and gentlemen, please give a warm welcome to Great Southern!" With that, Betts and his bandmates kicked in, and the music echoed around the greenroom. The band was playing literally six feet above us. We could feel their bass drum pounding in our chests.

About fifteen minutes into the show, the caterer came into the greenroom holding deli trays and placed them on the table. Next, he brought a large tub of ice, filled with two six-packs of Budweiser and some water. It's important that you remember this combination of refreshments.

The radio manager asked the caterer, "Do you mind if we grab a beer?"

"Well, I wouldn't," the caterer snapped. "This beer is for the band."

After the caterer left, the manager ignored the warning and headed for the beer tub. "I'm sure that Dickey Betts won't mind if we have a beer." So he grabbed two bottles, handed one to me, and we resumed our conversation.

Above us, Great Southern chugged on, sprinkling in some of Dickey's Allman Brothers hits like "Ramblin' Man," "Jessica" and "Blue Sky." While the band stomped overhead, I outlined my vision, and I could tell that I was scoring some points. Or maybe he was so buzzed that anything sounded good. At times, I had to yell to be heard above the music.

After an hour of talking, our throats were dry. So we each grabbed a second beer, then a third.

KISW's general manager and I continued talking and drinking as we got to know each other. The beer relaxed us both, and we were totally on the same page. I could taste the PD job. Or maybe it was the beer coming back up. When it comes to alcohol, I'm a lightweight.

Suddenly, the music stopped above us. We heard the crowd cheering and figured that Great Southern had finished their set. Too bad that we didn't get to see them play. But we sure heard them. Even though we were under the stage, I could still feel the ringing in my fillings. Soon, we heard five pairs of boots clomping down the stairs and headed our way. Great Southern marched into the greenroom soaked in sweat. They'd played for two hours, and now it was time to put down a few cold beers. They walked straight for the tubs and rummaged through the ice water. Much to their surprise, all of the Budweisers were gone. All that we'd left for them were bottles of water. Dickey Betts walked over to us and snarled, "Did you assholes drink our beer?" Judging by the dozen empty bottles at our feet, it was pretty clear that we had. We were caught red-handed and just sat there grinning like fools. Another band member chimed in, "Who the fuck gave you permission to drink our beer?" These good old boys were pissed. Hot, sweaty, thirsty and pissed. They continued to paw through the plastic tubs, hoping to find a Budweiser hidden under the ice. But there were none to be found. "We're sorry" wasn't going to cut it. Betts stared me down, and I needed to think fast. "I'll go find the caterer," I volunteered. "Maybe he has some more beer stashed away." I hated to leave my partner in crime alone with an angry band, but I was trying to save both of us from getting our asses kicked.

I stood up too quickly and almost toppled over. But I was on a mission. I ignored my wobbly legs and frantically ran through the hallways until I found the caterer. Thankfully, he had saved two more six-packs and pulled them out of the refrigerator. I grabbed one in each hand and ran back to Great Southern's greenroom. I walked in to find Dickey and the boys standing with their arms folded, surrounding KISW's manager. I pulled out the chilled beer bottles and handed them to Dickey. This pleased him for the moment, just long enough for me and my drinking buddy to make a quick exit.

Once outside the theater, the GM extended his hand and said, "I'd like to offer you the job of KISW program director." I stared at him through beer goggles and gladly accepted.

Maybe the alcohol clouded his judgment. Maybe he liked my quick thinking and resourcefulness. Or maybe he just liked my ability to find beer. But in the end, I got the job, Dickey Betts got his beer, and no one got hurt.

Chapter 18

ROBERT PLANT
AND THE HEDGEHOG

"If there's a bustle in your hedgerow, don't be alarmed
now. It's just a spring clean for the May queen."

Led Zeppelin "Stairway To Heaven"

Google the phrase "Rock God" and you will probably see a
picture of Robert Plant.

Famous for his tight leather pants, long golden curls and
hairy chest, Plant swung the hammer of the gods as the
front man for Led Zeppelin. He was the testosterone-
charged poster boy for heavy rock. Robert Plant was the
gold standard by which all rock stars would be compared.
Many singers tried to emulate him. But nobody could match
the singer's swagger or commanding stage presence.

After Led Zeppelin called it quits, Plant stepped down from
his throne and released a solo album called *Shaken 'n'
Stirred*. For the first time, he used different musicians and
embarked on a concert tour without his Zeppelin bandmates. Just the mention of seeing Robert Plant sent shiv-
ers down the spines of all Zeppelin fans. When he announced his first nationwide U.S. tour, his concerts sold
out quickly.

A few days before Plant's local show, his record company
rep called with an offer I couldn't refuse. "Robert doesn't

usually meet people. But if you'd like, I can bring you backstage for a private chat with him before the show."

"Are you kidding me? I'd love to meet Robert Plant!"

My friend went on, "Robert wants to hear how fans are responding to his new album. He wonders if they accept him as a solo artist."

I think I wet myself. "Cool! Yes! Absolutely! Wow!"

While I've met quite a few rock gods, I had yet to meet anyone from Led Zeppelin. Here was my chance to check "meet Robert Plant" off of my bucket list. I was thrilled, but also nervous. No matter how many stars you meet, it's intimidating to be face-to-face with your heroes. I'd be lying if I didn't admit that I get tongue-tied like anybody else. I usually mumble something stupid like "good show" or "you were great, really great." And then I retreat to a dark corner.

On the night of the concert, I was determined to impress Robert Plant. This time, I'd ask smart questions and not come across like a dork. Robert was due to take the stage in thirty minutes. So, his record company rep handed me a backstage pass and escorted me back to Plant's dressing room. We knocked, and an enormous security guard opened the door. I expected to see sleazy groupies, piles of booze bottles, and the full display of rock star decadence. Instead, the room was almost bare and quite understated. There were a few armchairs and a table filled with a selection of healthy food, as well as beer and wine. I joked to the label rep, "This looks too civilized. Are you sure we're not in Donny Osmond's room?"

I stepped inside and waited for a few minutes while nibbling from Plant's deli tray. Then, a side door opened—and there he was. Led Zeppelin's golden god glided to the center of the room. His shirt was unbuttoned to the navel, revealing a gold medallion nestled in a hairy, golden chest. Before I could say anything, he stuck out his hand and introduced himself: "Hi, I'm Robert Plant." As if I didn't know. Instead of swigging from a bottle of Jack Daniels, Plant looked refined, sipping a glass of white wine. He has a powerful aura about him, a supreme confidence. Being a few feet away, it was impossible not to feel that I was in the presence of greatness. The record company rep introduced me as we shook hands and cameras flashed. I asked Robert how he felt about touring without his partner in crime, Jimmy Page. He explained how excited he was to show more of a rhythmic side to fans and seemed ready to put Led Zeppelin behind him. I told Robert how our listeners loved his new album, and he beamed.

Our chat had been going pretty well. Now came my big moment. I was going to dazzle Robert Plant with my brilliance. So, I looked him in the eye and asked, "Robert, there's a line in 'Stairway To Heaven' that's always puzzled me. Can you explain it?"

"Sure, what's the line, mate?" he asked.

Eager to demonstrate my rock acumen, I blurted out, "What does it mean when you sing 'if there's a bustle in your *hedgehog*'?"

As soon as the words left my lips, I wished I could've pulled them back. Did I really say *hedgehog*? What the hell was I thinking? I've heard "Stairway To Heaven" a million times and know the lyrics by heart. As everyone knows, it's "hedge*row*." But my nerves got the best of me, and I blurted out the wrong word. I felt my knees buckle and my face flush with embarrassment. He must think I'm an imbecile!

Plant leaned back and laughed, then shook his head. "No man, it's hedge*row*, not hedge*hog*!" More laughing. If I only could slink away.

"Of course," I assured him. "I didn't mean to say hedgehog. I knew that." Geezus, this was my big chance to impress Led Zeppelin's golden god. Instead, I humiliated myself.

Unfazed, Plant explained. "In the springtime, haven't you noticed the birds nesting and singing in the bushes? In England, we call them hedgerows."

I turned nine shades of crimson. "Yes, of course. Birds in the hedges. I completely get it. Thanks Robert."

Now, can somebody please open a trap door and make me vanish?

C'mon mate...hedgehog? Really? What an idiot!

Chapter 19

JEFF BECK:
HERE & THERE & BACK

"If you were to plot my success or failure, it very
seldom stays on a high plateau."

Jeff Beck

Jeff Beck ranks among the greatest guitarists of all time. He
is true British rock royalty. But despite being a brilliant musician, Jeff Beck never earned the acceptance or success of
his peers. He has won several Grammy Awards and been
inducted into the Rock and Roll Hall of Fame twice. He
placed fifth on *Rolling Stone*'s list of the "100 Greatest Guitarists of All Time" (behind Hendrix and Clapton). Ironically,
Beck replaced Eric Clapton in the Yardbirds. But Jeff Beck
may go down in history as the Rodney Dangerfield of guitar
heroes. He never enjoyed the recognition or respect of his
fellow guitar greats.

And this incident didn't help.

In the summer of 1980, Jeff Beck released an album titled
There & Back. The title implies that this veteran guitarist has
seen it all during his long career. He played with everyone
from Rod Stewart to Mick Jagger, Roger Waters, Bon Jovi
and ZZ Top. With this new record, Jeff Beck moved away
from mainstream rock to jazz fusion. Despite the pleas from
his label Epic Records, KISW didn't play Jeff Beck's new album. To our ears, it just didn't fit on our meat and potatoes

rock station. Jazz fusion wasn't our thing, so we politely passed on *There & Back.*

In fact, many rock stations felt the same way and boycotted *There & Back.* This created a challenge for Epic, which relied on influential stations to get airplay and ultimately sell albums. So Jeff's record label came back with a new approach. They thought if I saw Jeff perform in concert, I'd be more open to playing his album. Then they sweetened the deal by inviting me backstage to meet Jeff before the show. How could I refuse?

I got to the show an hour early, and the Epic Records rep led me backstage. She was petite, but feisty, making her presence known with the backstage crew. She talked up a storm as we navigated the concrete tunnels that led to Jeff Beck's dressing room. The label rep knocked twice, and we entered a small, rectangular room that resembled a holding cell. Imagine cinder-block walls painted the color of toothpaste and bathed in fluorescent light. As we entered the room, Beck and his manager stepped forward to greet me. We shook hands and had a friendly chat for a few minutes. Beck was very gracious and reserved. Like Clapton and Page, he prefers to let his guitar do the talking.

When there was a lull in the conversation, the label rep changed the subject. "Everyone at Epic Records is so proud of your *Here & There* album, Jeff. In fact, we created 5,000 commemorative pins for tonight's show." She proudly handed a handful to Beck and his manager. She beamed, "Right now, our staff is outside passing out pins to the fans waiting in line."

"Hmmm," the manager mumbled. "So you're saying that everyone in the crowd tonight will be wearing a *Here & There* button?" Jeff Beck and his manager looked at the pins in their hands and then stared at each other in disbelief.

Using his most diplomatic English restraint, Beck's manager responded, "Well, that's very kind of you to produce these buttons for Jeff. Do they all say *Here & There*?"

The Epic rep boasted, "Yes, the buttons include Jeff's name, today's date and the *Here & There* album title."

The manager calmly listened, then dropped the hammer. "But that's not the correct album title, is it?"

"Uhhh, what?" was the best response the rep could muster, her face growing flush.

The manager's tone became more direct as his impatience grew. "I'm sure you realize that Jeff's new album is called *There & Back,* not *Here & There.* Do you understand the difference? *There & Back* is about Jeff's life journey, his amazing career dating back to the sixties. *Here & There* means nothing…except that this album is a joke. It makes his album sound frivolous. So by handing out 5,000 pins with the wrong title, you've made Mr. Beck look foolish."

Ouch. Beck's manager let her have it—in a mannered, English style. In mere seconds, the air went out of the room. The Epic rep was reeling like she'd run into an open propeller. She visibly slumped at the realization that she'd made a colossal screw-up and insulted a legendary artist. I could almost see the wheels turning in the rep's head. "What can I do? How can I make this right?" she must have wondered. But there was no excuse to be made, no way to fix the misprinted buttons. She screwed up, big time. Beck's manager folded his arms and waited for a response. It was like time stopped. Standing in that room was beyond uncomfortable. I looked for any opportunity to bail. Beck stared at his manager while the manager bored in on the Epic rep. He finally broke the silence with, "What do you plan to do about this?"

The label rep answered with the only thing she could think of: "What would you like me to do?"

Beck's manager snapped, "Here's what I'd like you to do," pointing a finger at her. He commanded, "Collect all of those buttons that you handed out. All of them. Get them back from people tonight. Tell the fans that you'll reprint the buttons with the correct title and hand out new pins to them ASAP. I don't care how. Just get it done now." The Epic rep froze. It wasn't realistic to take back thousands of pins as fans left the building. But this wasn't the time for excuses.

Check please!

During the awkward silence, I backed away and said my goodbyes. I thanked everyone for inviting me to the show and wished Jeff good luck. This was going to end badly, so I found the closest exit. On a personal level, it was a thrill to meet Jeff Beck.

But we still didn't play his album

1. STAR CYCLE (4:56)
2. TOO MUCH TO LOSE (2:55)
3. YOU NEVER KNOW (4:03)
4. THE PUMP (5:43)
5. EL BECKO (3:59)
6. THE GOLDEN ROAD (4:55)
7. SPACE BOOGIE (5:04)
8. THE FINAL PEACE (3:36)

Co-Produced by Jeff Beck and Ken Scott
Recorded in London, England

Package Design & Photography by John Berg
1980 CBS Inc. / 1980 CBS Inc./Manufactured by Epic Records/CBS Inc./51 W. 52 Street, New York, NY/"Epic," are trademarks of CBS Inc. throughout the world except in Canada where they are trademarks of CBS Records Canada Ltd. Printed in U.S.A./WARNING: All Rights Reserved. Unauthorized duplication is a violation of applicable laws.

Chapter 20

TED NUGENT, MOTOR CITY MADMAN

"For the Nugent family, fast food is a running herbivore."

Ted Nugent

Before Ted Nugent was a bow-huntin', gun-lovin', Tea-Partyin' reality TV star, he was a guitar slinger extraordinaire. Ted was bombastic in concert, the consummate showman. He knew what his fans wanted and served it up with te subtlety of a jackhammer. Nugent's often perverted songs were devoured by millions of young guys...and only the toughest women.

"The Nuge" loved being a rock & roll caricature and reveled in being the center of attention. In his heyday, Ted Nugent was a one-man gang with an assortment of nicknames including "Terrible Ted," "the Motor City Madman," "Uncle Ted" and my favorite, "the Master of Disaster." His brand of Detroit hard rock had only one gear—fast. Ted was famous for tender love songs like "Yank Me, Crank Me," "Wang Dang Sweet Poontang" and "Wango Tango." Every day was a new opportunity for Ted to be even more outrageous.

During his 1981 American tour, Ted Nugent opened his shows with a memorable entrance. Most artists just walk on stage to start their concerts. Not Terrible Ted. Each night, he'd climb to the top of a fifteen-foot stack of speakers and grab a rope attached from the scaffolding above. Then, doing his best Tarzan impersonation, he'd leap off and swing across the stage to the delight of his fans. Wearing only a loincloth, Uncle Ted would drop to the stage and grab his hunting bow. As fans watched in awe, Nugent would light the tip of an arrow and shoot it at his guitar. The guitar would erupt in flames as Nugent raised his arms in triumph, celebrating his kill. Ted never missed. Was there a message behind torching a guitar with a flaming arrow? Who cares? Ted could do no wrong, and his fans ate it up.

Technically, radio and TV stations are forbidden from airing foul language. But when an event is live, the rules are a bit vague—it's impossible to predict what might be said or done during a live broadcast. Janet Jackson's wardrobe malfunction during the Super Bowl halftime show in 2004 is a case in point. The FCC ruled against CBS Television and fined them a record $550,000 for the "Nipplegate" incident. But that fine was appealed and ultimately overturned seven years later.

In 1981, Ted Nugent's guitars were loud, his hair was big, and his language was filthy. Knowing his propensity for cursing at will, I foolishly suggested an idea to Nugent's record label. "All of the tickets to Ted's Seattle concert sold out in a few hours. So, thousands of his fans won't get to see him play." I wound up for my big pitch: "What if my radio station did a live simulcast of Ted's show?"

I could hear the hesitation in the record rep's voice. "You know, Ted gets a little crazy onstage. And his language can be…uh, colorful. Are you sure that you want to put that on your radio station, live?"

He was right, of course. But I knew that the excitement of a live Ted Nugent radio concert would be the talk of the town and surely boost our ratings. On the other hand, I knew that Nugent would swear like a drunken sailor. But I had a plan for that. A way to keep our station from incurring the wrath of the FCC.

I couldn't risk a battle with the FCC. If we didn't handle this broadcast by the book, the morality police could revoke our broadcasting license or clobber the station with staggering fines. A live, uncensored Ted Nugent broadcast was not for the faint of heart. I knew I was asking for trouble and walking on the razor's edge. But I pressed on because of the dazzling payoff. I conferred with our station manager and legal counsel. I leveled with them, saying, "There will be swearing during the concert.

There were no "dump" buttons back then. No seven-second delays. So our only option was to air the show as it happened and take our chances.

And there is no way to edit or bleep Nugent. Whatever Ted says onstage will be heard by 350,000 radio listeners. How can we simulcast the concert without losing our license?"

Our attorney suggested, "What if you run disclaimer announcements throughout the day, leading up to the 8 p.m. simulcast? If you air them on the station every hour, you can warn listeners about the 'potential for profanity' in Ted Nugent's concert. In other words, give people a heads-up so they won't be shocked."

Great idea. So I went to work and crafted an announcement that read:

Tonight at 8 p.m., this station will broadcast Ted Nugent's sold-out concert. The show will be simulcast live and un-

censored. It may include profane language. If this makes you feel uncomfortable, please do not listen tonight from 8 p.m. until 10 p.m. And if you choose to tune in for this broadcast, please keep children out of the room. We cannot be held responsible for what Ted Nugent might say during this live concert.

From a purely legal standpoint, our station made an honest effort to act responsibly. At least that was our rationale. Of course, airing those disclaimers only added fuel to the fire and created more anticipation. Those who might be offended had been duly warned. Meanwhile, our loyal listeners would make a point to listen.

At the Ted Nugent concert that night, I walked into the sound truck to make sure that our station was ready to receive whatever Ted dished out. With my heart in my throat and career on the line, I headed back into the concert hall. In a few moments, I would turn over my radio station to the Motor City Madman.

Standing near the stairs to the stage, I saw Ted Nugent heading my way. In true Ted form, he was naked, except for a small loincloth. At that moment, the house lights went down, the crowd screamed, and lighters were raised overhead. Ted walked up to me, put his arm on my shoulder and yelled in my ear, "I hope you don't expect me to change my show just because it's being simulcast on your radio station." He grinned and added, "So get ready."

The color drained from my face. I knew what was coming next. But before I could respond, Ted bolted up the stairs to the stage, his loincloth flapping against his ass cheeks. Before the spotlight could find him, Nugent climbed to the top of the speakers and grabbed the rope that would propel him on stage. He flung himself off the fifteen-foot high stack and swung out across the stage to the delight of his fans.

144

Ted jumped off the rope at center stage, picked up his hunting bow, and fired a flaming arrow across the stage. True to form, the arrow pierced the heart of his guitar, causing it to burst into flames. The Nuge raised his arms like Rocky Balboa and strolled around the stage, drinking in the roar of approval from his fans.

Then, the Motor City Madman grabbed the microphone and announced to the concert crowd (and my radio listeners), "I came here tonight for two reasons."

Uh-oh. C'mon Ted, be nice. Don't start getting dirty yet.

"First," yelled Nugent, "I came here to eat as much Seattle pussy as I can."

Sweet Jesus. Just one minute into the concert and my stomach hit the floor.

"And second, I came to rock your balls off."

The Master of Disaster wasted no time in testing the FCC's tolerance. He had the crowd in the palm of his hand and played it to the hilt. Fifteen minutes later, Nugent looked over at me and winked as he grabbed the mic.

"Anybody want to get mellow?" Ted asked, as I felt another shiver down my spine.

The crowd hollered back in unison, "Noooooo!"

"Well if anyone wants to get mellow, you can get the fuck out of here!"

I shuddered at the thought of an f-bomb blasting through KISW's 100,000-watt transmitter. But there was no turning back. For the next two hours, my radio station broadcasted a blistering live set from Terrible Ted, punctuated with every curse word imaginable. And then some.

I felt very alone. The concert promoter moved away from me, as did my staff and the record label rep who'd warned me. I got myself into this mess by requesting a live simulcast. Now I was left to live with the consequences—and twist in the wind.

Nugent slammed through his set to the delight of the crowd. For two hours, he paraded around the stage while his loincloth flapped in the breeze. "Cat Scratch Fever" gave fans an adrenaline rush; the tender "Stranglehold" and the romantic "Yank Me, Crank Me" followed. Ted didn't miss any chances to take the low road and cursed at will. The crowd was on its feet—while I was on my ass. I took a gamble and should have known better. I was in no mood to go backstage after the show. I couldn't blame Nugent. He was just being Terrible Ted. This was my screw-up. On the drive home, I convinced myself this was the final stake in my radio career.

The following morning, I expected to be greeted by a blizzard of complaints. So, I drove into the station early to meet my fate head on. I was clinging to my only defense: that we'd warned listeners in advance. Before anyone else arrived, I snuck in through the side door and hid in my office. I sat in there in the darkness, just staring at the phone, waiting for the missiles headed my way.

My phone was silent. The message light wasn't flashing, but I checked anyway. None. And no parents' groups were picketing outside. Amazingly, there was no fallout from Nugent's profanity-laced concert broadcast. Zero. Maybe it was because of our pre-show announcements that warned people not to listen if they were easily offended. While that message kept us legally in the clear, it also helped us attract rock fans like moths to a flamethrower. We might as well have said, "If you want to hear Ted drop f-bombs on the radio, be listening tonight at 8 p.m."

To my surprise (and relief), KISW received no complaints about Ted Nugent's offensive language. Not one angry parent sent a letter claiming that I corrupted their children. No advertisers canceled their ads over this obscene stunt. I got to keep my job a little longer. And our lawyers lost out on a hefty payday.

Hanging out with Ted Nugent and KISW's Gary Crow & Steve Slaton a few hours before our live broadcast

Chapter 21

GETTING KINKY
WITH ZZ TOP

"I got a girl, she lives cross town.
She's the one that really gets down when she boogie.
She do the tube snake boogie."

ZZ Top "Tube Snake Boogie"

In 1984, ZZ Top was the coolest band on the planet. It seemed like every radio station was wearing out the grooves of their super-smooth *Eliminator* album. And back when MTV played videos, those bearded dudes had the formula down cold. ZZ Top's sexy videos for "Legs,", "Sharp Dressed Man," and "Gimme All Your Lovin' " were all over MTV. Each featured grinding songs, grinding women and a cherry red 1933 coupe. This band had a sense of humor to match their sense of style. When ZZ Top hit the road, it was a Southern-fried party on wheels. They may look like hillbillies, but that "Little Ol' Band from Texas" partied like rock stars.

I had a friend who worked with ZZ Top's management company. One day he called to say, "ZZ is coming to Seattle next week, and the band is staying at a hotel near the airport. Why don't you come by after the show and hang out with us?"

"Sounds great. I'd love to." I was curious to see how the guys from ZZ Top entertained themselves after hours.

They've had a kinky reputation since their first single "Salt Lick," which goes, "She had a time gettin' down to work, with a salt lick in her hand." Didn't sound like the kind of salt licks they use to feed wild animals.

For just three guys, ZZ Top makes a loud racket in concert. Their show was a multimedia experience, with clips of their flame-red roadster roaring across giant TV screens. Meanwhile, onstage, guitarist Billy Gibbons stood shoulder-to-shoulder with bassist Dusty Hill, both looking dapper in cowboy hats and wraparound shades. Their long beards swayed to the beat, perfectly synchronized. I was watching the show from the press box in the center of the arena when the door opened to our small room. I smelled food. At that moment, ZZ Top kicked into their song "TV Dinners," as their record label passed out piping hot TV dinners to the dozen or so guests.

ZZ Top concerts were famously outrageous. During their Worldwide Texas Tour, six animals paraded around the stage — a longhorn steer, a 2,000-pound black buffalo, two trained black buzzards, and two huge rattlesnakes. The band traveled with a veterinarian and reportedly spent $140,000 to insure the animals' health.

After the show, I drove to the airport hotel, parked in the hotel lot, and headed for the lobby. I was thinking about all the ZZ Top songs written about kinky sex, and here I was going to their hotel room. I had no idea what to expect. Orgies? Livestock? Inside the elevator, I punched the penthouse button, then got off at the top floor. As I approached the double doors at the end of the hallway, I heard music coming from the suite. I knocked, and my friend opened the door, just enough to poke his head out. He looked down the left hallway, then the right. When he was convinced the coast was clear, he stepped outside of the room, closed the door behind him and whispered, "Look, it's getting freaky in there. Billy, Dusty and Frank (Beard) are doing an interview with the number-one Japanese music interviewer. They say he's the Dick Clark of Japan."

"No problem," I said.

"Uhhh, and there's some wild girls inside the suite. They're really perverted," he added.

"Whatever. I'd expect that from a band that writes songs like "Pearl Necklace." Don't worry, I'm a big boy," I assured my friend. "I've seen it all. So, I won't be shocked." He opened the door a bit wider to let me in, and we stepped inside the suite. Okay, I was shocked.

ZZ Top's three amigos were sprawled out on couches, wrapped in white hotel bathrobes. Two Asian men were sitting in armchairs across from the band. One of them held a microphone. I assumed he was the honorable "Dick Clark." His assistant/interpreter stood behind Dick, holding a clipboard. The Asians were dressed in dark suits and looked totally out of their element. Clearly this was their first time in the hotel room of an American rock band, where dress is casual and clothes are optional. These reporters were in for a special treat.

ZZ Top's penthouse suite was huge, with floor-to-ceiling glass walls offering a sweeping view. In the center of the room were three hot, young women—no doubt some new friends the band had brought back from the concert. The young ladies were naked and squirming on the floor, performing for the band's pleasure. The girls were crawling all over one another, hands groping, and licking each other from head to toe. The Japanese Dick Clark was having difficulty focusing on the interview. He reached into his lapel pocket, grabbed a crisp hankie and dabbed his forehead before continuing. "Are your beards…uuuh…real?" he asked distractedly, as the women moaned with pleasure on the carpet.

"Want to touch it and check for yourself?" joked Gibbons. But the interviewer, with one eye on ZZ Top and the other riveted on the women, didn't hear Billy's answer. I thought his eyeballs would pop out of his head. The geisha girls in Japan were nothing like this.

Trying to regain his composure, the honorable Dick Clark asked, "Tell me about your music videos. How do you…" As his words trailed off, it was clear that he'd lost all interest in the interview. Asian Dick finally surrendered and set his microphone down so he could fully concentrate on the writhing mass of sex. Both Japanese guests were now fixated on the groupies and sporting shit-eating grins. In fairness, they weren't alone. I stood near the windows enjoying the three-way action, while the three bearded dudes smiled and took it all in.

About twenty minutes later, the ladies untangled themselves and turned their attention toward Billy, Dusty and Frank. They crawled toward the boys on the couch and opened their robes. If the Japanese Dick Clark hadn't asked all of his questions by now, he'd lost his chance. The three hombres excused themselves, then each grabbed a girl and headed for a bedroom. The living room floor show was over, and the party was now moving behind closed doors.

The Asian reporters looked dazed as they gathered up their recording gear, not sure what they'd just seen. Welcome to America, Dick Clark-san.

Chapter 22

WHO FIRED
JIMMY KIMMEL?

"I always think my boss is going to think something I do
is funny. And usually they don't."

Jimmy Kimmel

The funniest radio DJs are always on in the morning.
Whether they're hosting solo or a full-blown morning zoo,
it's their job to make you smile and jumpstart your day. Stations go to great lengths to find entertaining people to anchor their morning drive shows. Radio program directors
mix and match DJs (aka jocks) with local comedians and
even regular folks. I once hired a guy for a morning show
who ran a coffee cart in front of Nordstrom. What can I say?
He was funny.

In 1986, KISW's morning show featured a feisty, potty-
mouthed woman and her bizarro sidekick. A perfect match
for a rock station, they were insanely popular and kicked-
butt in the all-important ratings. Our main competitor,
KZOK, had churned through a steady stream of morning
hosts, trying to find a team that had chemistry. But none of
them made a dent in the ratings or even lasted a year. Not
even a young, aspiring DJ named Jimmy Kimmel.

My pal Larry Sharp was the program director of KZOK at the
time. Not surprisingly, he was looking to hire a new morning
show when his boss called and said, "Larry, I'm sending you

an aircheck from a morning team in Phoenix called 'Me & Him.' I think they're pretty funny. Please listen to their demo and let me know what you think. I'll call you next week."

A few days later, the demo tape arrived from "Me & Him." Sharp popped it into his cassette machine and hoped these guys would be the answer to his morning show prayers.

If you don't know what a cassette is, you were probably born after 1990.

After listening to the demo, Sharp's hopes were dashed. He recalls, "My first reaction was that these two guys weren't funny. Neither 'Me' or 'Him' made me laugh. They just sounded like two guys cracking each other up. But my boss must have heard something special or he wouldn't have recommended them. So I listened to their tape again—and it still wasn't funny."

When Sharp's boss called the following week, he asked "So, what did you think of the 'Me & Him' show?"

"Not much," Larry responded. "I listened to their demo twice. But they're just not what I'm looking for."

"Hmmm. That's too bad," his boss grumbled. "I just hired 'Me & Him' for your station. They start on Monday. In fact, they're driving to Seattle as we speak. They're probably halfway there."

Picking up the story from there, Sharp remembers, "When I met Jimmy Kimmel, he was a cocky 19-year-old kid. He was constantly doing goofy shit on-air, like playing the banjo and making up stupid lyrics, or doing bad Dick Vitale impressions. I tried to help Jimmy. But he ignored my direction at every turn and just did whatever he wanted. We had totally different ideas on what was funny."

After "Me & Him" got off the air at 10 a.m., Larry would pull Kent and Jimmy into his office to discuss the show. Sharp remembers, "I'd play back Jimmy's segment from that morning and we'd listen together. He would be cracking up, laughing at his own jokes. All I heard was lame attempts at humor, and I finally told him it wasn't that funny. Kimmel would snap back with, 'You don't know what's funny! Who made you the arbiter of funny?' "

Larry recalls having regular meetings with Voss and Kimmel after their show. "Jimmy didn't like our critique sessions and wasn't shy about letting me know. To piss me off, he would come into my office, sit down and prop up his feet on my desk. Kimmel was clearly provoking me. He would do it every day, just to show disrespect."

One day, Jimmy pushed too hard. Sharp recalls, "Jimmy came into my office for our meeting and put his shoes up on my desk. I had come to expect that and let it go.

Radio veteran Kent Voss, half of KZOK's "Me & Him" show, offers more of the backstory: "I was doing the afternoon show in Phoenix with another guy. Jimmy Kimmel was a student at Arizona State University who used to call the show and do bits. I met him at a station appearance at Houlihan's, I think. He used a fake ID to get in. Jimmy was a funny guy, and we started to hang out. Shortly after, I left Phoenix and got a chance to do mornings at KZOK in Seattle. The brain trust there asked if there was somebody that I wanted to work with as my partner. So, I said, 'Yeah, I know this guy named Jimmy Kimmel who would be great.' So, Jimmy and I made an aircheck and drove to Seattle, replacing a morning show called 'The Oatmeal Buddies.' "

But when I looked at his feet, I noticed there were words scribbled on the soles of Kimmel's shoes. I leaned in and read his personal message to me. Jimmy watched my reaction as I read his On the bottom of one shoe he'd written 'Fuck,' and the other read 'You.' Jimmy watched my reaction as I read his shoes, and laughed."

With that, Sharp stopped trying to be Mr. Nice Guy. He let Kimmel have it, which only made things worse. "I tried everything with Jimmy. But dealing with him was brutal. He would slam me by name on the air. He even read my private memos to him during his show for everyone to hear. Kimmel thought it was outrageously funny. That made one of us. When the general manager wrote a personal note to Kimmel, he'd read that out loud, too." Sharp was exasperated and finally had enough. "Our morning ratings sucked, so I fired both 'Me' and 'Him.' They were out of work for a while before landing at a radio station in Tampa. I heard Jimmy got fired there too."

In the months that followed, a stream of comedians passed through Larry Sharp's radio station. Many of them were friends with Kimmel. "It's amazing how many comics knew me as the guy who fired Jimmy," Sharp remembers. "They told me that Kimmel loved telling the story of his f-you shoes." Sharp is more philosophical. "I think Jimmy wanted to get fired. Making me the bad guy helped spur him on. Yeah, that's it. When I canned Jimmy Kimmel, he had something to prove. I really did him a favor!"

After several years of bouncing around as a morning DJ, Kimmel left radio behind and quickly gained attention on television as a guest on *Win Ben Stein's Money*. Then, Jimmy got his own show as co-host of *The Man Show* alongside Adam Carolla. Now of course, he is the host of *Jimmy Kimmel Live!* and is a Hollywood star.

Riding high as a national TV celebrity, Kimmel returned to his radio roots four years after the KZOK debacle as a keynote speaker at the annual Radio & Records luncheon in Los Angeles. The ballroom was filled with about 1500 broadcasters. A who's who of top radio execs from around the country gathered. Everyone was excited to hear one of radio's most famous alums describe his meteoric rise to fame. Jimmy Kimmel, a failure on the "Me & Him" show, was returning with tablets of wisdom.

Jimmy was introduced and confidently strode across the stage to a standing ovation. He settled in behind the podium and gazed out over the audience. Amidst the sea of "suits," Kimmel found a familiar face— his ex-boss Larry Sharp—and for a moment their eyes locked. Jimmy stood at center stage, welcomed the crowd and told a few jokes. Then, he continued, "When I started in radio, I worked in Seattle for a program director named Larry Sharp. Larry, I know that you're here today. Please stand up and say hi, Larry."

Sharp knew exactly where this was going and wisely kept his seat. "I knew that Jimmy would skewer me, so there was no way I was going to stand up", he relates.

Kimmel wouldn't let it go. "Larry, I know that you're out there. C'mon, stand up."

"I slid down in my chair, hoping that nobody would notice me," Sharp admits. "I wanted to disappear. But other guys at my table were looking at me and encouraging me to stand up. No way. Not gonna happen."

Kimmel went for the kill. "Larry Sharp was the first asshole to ever fire me. He always told me that I'm not funny. Well look at me now, motherfucker. My car is worth more than your damn house!"

The crowd roared, and even Larry Sharp had to laugh.

After Kimmel left the stage, he bumped into Sharp near the exit. Jimmy pulled Larry aside and offered a sheepish apology, of sorts: "Sorry, man. At least *this* audience thought I was funny!"

Chapter 23

BRIAN JOHNSON's
FAVORITE SHIRT

"We just go out and don't give a fuck about critics.
We play what we play and that's that."

Brian Johnson

In rock's glory days, Australia was home to the hottest band that you've never heard of. They were called the Angels, known in America as Angel City. Their leader, Doc Neeson, was a six-foot-five-inch singer with a punk rock edge, reminiscent of the Clash's Joe Strummer. Angel City and AC/DC were often mentioned in the same breath in Australia, both vying for the crown of the best rock band from Down Under. But while Angel City was wildly popular at home, they lived in AC/DC's shadow in the U.S. and never broke through.

When artists went on tour, it was common practice for them to visit the local rock stations while in

Seattle was the one of the few American cities where Angel City had a following. My radio station loved the band and played several of their songs. As the reaction from listeners heated up, we worked with their record label to bring Doc and Angel City to town for a Rising Star concert in 1980. Tickets were just $2 and sold out in a few hours.

town. Band members frequently came to KISW and raided our prize closet. They loved wearing our black T-shirts with the bold yellow Rock logo. Both AC/DC's Brian Johnson and Angel City's Doc Neeson were avid swag collectors, and both singers owned a KISW shirt. We never dreamed that might cause a problem.

Brian Johnson, AC/DC's gravel-voiced singer, told me this story: "A few months after I joined AC/DC, we went on tour. We wanted to show fans that the band was back in black, as they say. After playing concerts all over the world, our final gig was in Australia. Even though I'd played eighty shows with the boys, I was nervous about playing in front of AC/DC's hometown fans. After all, they have to *live* there."

Brian continued, "AC/DC was booked to play a big music festival in Sydney and we were co-headlining with the Angels. So, we wanted to put on a great show and outdo them. Australians love both AC/DC and Angel City. But we've got a friendly rivalry, and their singer Doc Neeson is a good mate. We both like to wear T-shirts from American rock stations onstage. On the day of the big festival, I was walking around backstage when I came upon Doc. We stopped and stared at each other in surprise. Doc and I both showed up wearing the *same* shirt, from KISW, a rock station in Seattle. We had a good laugh. And then he said, 'Well we both can't go on stage wearing the *same* T-shirt. So you'd better go back to your trailer and put on another shirt."

"I'm not changing my shirt, Doc," said Johnson. "I'm wearing this one."

The two singers mulled the situation. "Okay, I've got an idea," said Neeson. "Let's flip for it. Heads means you wear the shirt onstage. If it's tails, I'll wear it."

Listening to Brian Johnson tell the story, I felt honored just to hear that two hugely popular bands were having a tug-of-war over our shirt. While KISW valued our friendship with Angel City, AC/DC was the bigger band, by far. Having Johnson wearing our shirt in front of 50,000 people would be huge. So, as I listened to Brian tell about the winner-take-all coin flip, I was praying for a happy ending. Please God, let the coin land on heads.

Johnson's play-by-play continued: "So Doc tossed the coin in the air and it landed on heads. 'I win!' I yelled. Doc turned and headed back to his trailer to find a new shirt. And I went on stage wearing the KISW shirt."

Whew! Our promotion staff immediately went to work, trying to find a picture of Brian Johnson wearing the KISW shirt onstage in Sydney. After a lot of digging, they found the photograph we were seeking. It was published in a popular Japanese music magazine and clearly showed Brian Johnson wearing our T-shirt, flanked by a shirtless Angus Young. It was perfect. So, I contacted the Japanese magazine and offered to buy the film negative of their AC/DC picture. We cut a fair deal and got the band's permission to produce 10,000 posters.

The AC/DC posters featured the blown up image of Brian and Angus onstage at the Australian rock festival. The posters turned out beautifully, and we knew they'd sell quickly. So, we placed all 10,000 prints at the main Tower Records store in downtown Seattle and priced them at just $3 each. All proceeds would go to charity, but we hadn't decided which one. After two days, Tower called with the news that all of the posters had been sold—10,000 posters in forty-eight hours. It was the fastest selling poster in Tower's history.

KISW always wanted to have a relationship with the Children's Hospital of Seattle. Granted, we were strange bedfellows. But this was our chance to pay it forward and collaborate with the hospital. After a few conversations with the Children's administrator, we offered to donate the proceeds from our AC/DC poster sales to their music program. The band planned to be in town the following month. So, we held off presenting the check until AC/DC could join us in person.

The band and I drove to Children's Hospital and drew lots of stares as we entered the lobby. Clearly, this ragtag group wasn't a team of doctors. The Children's Hospital executives greeted AC/DC's band members warmly—and seemed clueless as to who they were. Prim, elegantly dressed execs stood alongside the reputed "bad boys from Down Under." I watched two worlds collide as the hospital administrators accepted a $30,000 check from guitar-slayer Angus Young.

In the end, everybody won. We harnessed the power of rock & roll to fund a music program that made the kids' hospital stays a bit brighter.

AC/DC presenting a $30,000
check to Children's Hospital,
the proceeds from our
poster sales

AC/DC

SEATTLE CENTER COLISEUM FEBRUARY 9, 10 & 11 1982.

KISW·FM 100

THIS 17" x 24" COLLECTABLE COLOR POSTER ON SALE NOW
FOR $3.00 AT ANY TOWER RECORDS.
PLUS EVERY AC/DC CATALOG ALBUM ON SALE!

Chapter 24

THE REBIRTH OF
BOB GELDOF

"Music is something I must do, business is something
I need to do, and Africa is something I have to do. "

Bob Geldof

The Boomtown Rats were an Irish band, led by charismatic
singer/songwriter Bob Geldof. Despite their valiant efforts,
the Rats never successfully infested America. But that didn't
stop Geldof from behaving like a rock star. Tall and ruggedly
handsome, he looked the part. Bob was the alpha male,
the Chief Rat, the bad boy, dressed in black. Onstage, he
loved being the center of attention. Bob wasn't blessed with
a great voice. But he snarled like Johnny Rotten and moved
like Jagger. However, the sad reality is that the Boomtown
Rats were a footnote in rock history.

That said, Bob Geldof is a superstar. Just not in the way
he'd hoped.

Geldof invited controversy wherever he went and seemed to
enjoy the conflict. Bob scoffed at conventional wisdom and
got off on challenging public opinion. This came to a head
after the Boomtown Rats released a song called "I Don't
Like Mondays" that documented a horrific shooting spree by
a 16-year-old girl. The girl fired at children in a school play-
ground in San Diego, killing two adults and injuring eight
kids, plus a police officer. During her trial, the girl showed

no remorse for her crime and explained, "I don't like Mondays. This livens up the day."

Geldof heard about this incident as he was doing a radio interview in Atlanta and was inspired to write a song. "I read the story as it came out of the telex machine beside me. Not liking Mondays as a reason for doing somebody in is a bit strange. So, I just said out loud that 'a silicon chip inside her head had switched to overload,' and I wrote that down."

The press raked Geldof and the Boomtown Rats over the coals, blasting them for exploiting an act of violence. Geldof fought back. "It wasn't an attempt to glorify a tragedy. Those killings were a perfectly senseless act. So perhaps I wrote the perfectly senseless song to illustrate it." Nonetheless, the media crucified Geldof and his band. It didn't help that Bob had an edge that could rub people the wrong way. He was strong-minded and probably did set out to write a provocative song. Still, the Rats faced a tidal wave of resentment and bad press.

When questioned about the meaning of "I Don't Like Mondays," Geldof appeared unfazed by the media criticism, perhaps because the song was immensely popular in England. In fact, "I Don't Like Mondays" was one of the biggest-selling singles in British music history. But the gun culture in England is a far cry from that in the U.S. After reeling from the San Diego shooting, Americans expected Geldof to appear more contrite and sympathetic. But that wasn't Bob's style. As a result, most American radio stations turned their backs on the Boomtown Rats and refused to play the song...except for my station. We felt that the Boomtown Rats were being characterized unfairly and refused to get swept up in the negative hysteria. It wasn't our role to play judge and jury. KISW's DJs talked openly about the Boomtown Rats situation on-air, and we let Geldof's music do the talking.

Of the 165 rock stations in America, mine was the Rats' only ally. Despite our success with playing "I Don't Like Mondays," other rock stations turned a deaf ear to the Boomtown Rats. To them, Bob Geldof would only attract negative controversy. They couldn't be bothered and wrote off the band. Meanwhile, my station addressed the "how could you play that song?" complaints and continued to play it. It was popular with our listeners, and KISW viewed this song as an artist's expression. Rock songs often make a statement, as evidenced by Neil Young's "Ohio" or

Columbia Records made a huge investment in the Boomtown Rats. They paid a fortune to secure the U.S. rights to the band's debut album. Columbia was committed to breaking the Rats in the U.S. and were desperate to get airplay on top rock stations.

the Who's "Won't Get Fooled Again." KISW stood behind the band and booked a Rising Star concert with the Boomtown Rats. It was the only show on their entire U.S. tour that sold out.

At the Rats concert, there was no opening band. Instead, we staged an air-guitar contest starring radio listeners who'd won local invisible-guitar competitions. Geldof and the band got into the spirit and entered the Boomtown Rats as air-guitar contestants. They finished fifth. Afterward, Geldof and company took the stage, this time with their instruments, and rocked the capacity crowd.

Ten days later, I saw Bob Geldof again. And things ended quite differently.

Jonathan Coffino, a VP with Columbia Records, needed a last gasp, Hail Mary pass to salvage the Boomtown Rats' career. They were getting almost no support from rock stations and started losing steam. Without radio airplay, the band had no chance. So, Coffino appealed to Lee Abrams, rock radio's top consultant, and convinced him to bring his most influential radio clients to see the Boomtown Rats perform. The band was scheduled to play a concert in...you guessed it, San Diego. The theater was located just miles away from the scene of the "I Don't Like Mondays" killing.

Columbia had one final chance to court the influential radio program directors who ran the biggest rock stations in America. Coincidentally, the PDs would be meeting in San Diego that same week, attending Abrams's annual conference. If Lee could deliver the top radio guys to the Boomtown Rats concert, Columbia offered to roll out the red carpet.

What could go wrong? Just about everything.

The Boomtown Rats were booked at a vintage, renovated theater in San Diego that held about 1,500 people. The show was open to the public on this historic night, and the theater was about half full. Coffino shifted nervously in the theater lobby, watching the crowd file in. He knew that tonight's Boomtown Rats performance would make or break them.

The guests of honor that evening were the elite group of radio programmers—twenty men bestowed with powers to grant life or death to hopeful new bands like the Boomtown Rats. And I was one of them. Each radio guy was decked out in his finest satin jacket. These shiny, colorful coats were awarded to radio PDs by record labels and artists. The radio guys wore them like badges of honor and strutted into the theater like peacocks on parade. Nineteen of the radio guys took their seats in the center of the tenth row. I chose not to be part of that scene and stood against the back wall of the lower level, with *Rolling Stone* magazine writer (and future filmmaker) Cameron Crowe.

The stage was set for a Shakespearean tragedy. Here were the players in this drama:

- The Boomtown Rats realized that this show was do-or-die. It was their last chance to get airplay on American radio stations. Geldof needed to get the crowd going and win over the jaded group of radio programmers. If the band wasn't convincing tonight, it was curtains.

- Columbia Records had bet heavily, and their investment in the Boomtown Rats was at stake. By bringing key radio decision-makers to this show, Columbia went all-in.

- After spending all day in conference rooms, the radio guys wanted to party. Instead, they were required to attend this Boomtown Rats concert.

In other words, the Boomtown Rats concert was doomed from the start.

The house lights dimmed and the Boomtown Rats took the stage. A tall and wiry Bob Geldof leapt around the stage and belted out a punky tune called "Rat Trap." I looked over at the satin-jacket section and saw that the programmers looked unimpressed.

About thirty minutes into the concert, Geldof stopped the music and grabbed the microphone. He said, "I've got something on my mind." I glanced over at Coffino, who looked on nervously, wondering what was coming next. Cameron Crowe and I were still standing in the back of the theater, and we watched as Bob pointed his finger at the group of radio execs and shook his head. He barked, "Hey, you, working the spotlight. I want you to shine it right down here. Shine the light on this group of American radio hotshots. Look at them," he spat. "All wearing their shiny satin jackets."

Okay, game on. This was getting good. The radio guys froze like frightened deer when the spotlight hit them. They were trapped in their seats, caught unawares. Cameron Crowe started scribbling notes as Geldof picked up the pace and got the crowd involved. "Let me ask you a question. What do you think of rock stations in America? Doesn't all of that corporate rock sound like shit?"

The crowd booed hard enough to shake the rafters. Fueled by their deafening roar, Geldof went for the jugular. "Well I'll tell you who's to blame for why radio sucks. It's *your* fault." Geldof stabbed his finger toward the group of radio guys, all seated together in the middle of the tenth row. The spotlight bore down on the nineteen peacocks and reflected off of their shimmering jackets. Man, was I glad I hadn't sat there. Geldof continued to tighten his noose and provoked the crowd with, "These guys are the ones responsible for the shitty music you hear on the radio. Tell them what you think of their stations!"

Another thundering blast of disapproval came from the crowd. The radio guys squirmed uncomfortably in their seats, with nowhere to hide. Geldof continued to scold them for a few excruciating minutes, but it felt like hours. We were witnessing rock history. A band was committing career suicide before our eyes.

After the show, I headed back to the hotel. Walking to my room, I thought I heard Jonathan Coffino's voice. As I walked down the hallway, his voice grew louder. The hotel room door was open, and I could see Jonathan yelling at someone. I poked my head in the doorway and saw Geldof sitting in a chair, slumped forward. Coffino was pacing back and forth and tearing into him. "Jesus, Bob. What the fuck were you thinking? I played my last card to get those radio programmers here tonight. And you insult them?" Geldof lowered his head as Jonathan piled it on. "Without help from those guys, you're screwed. You just killed your band in America, Bob. There's no way any of those radio stations will play the Boomtown Rats now. It's over."

The Boomtown Rats had put a nail in their American dream twenty-four hours earlier, ironically in San Diego. They triggered their own rat trap and snapped their necks in the process. The Rats were never to be heard from again.

But this story doesn't end here. In fact, this was just the beginning. While Geldof's singing career fizzled, he went on to enjoy tremendous international success. Geldof co-wrote the song "Do They Know It's Christmas? (Feed the World)," one of the best-selling singles of all time. And he starred in the film *Pink Floyd, The Wall.*

More notably, Bob Geldof became a political activist and one of the most celebrated humanitarians in the world. He is widely recognized for his anti-poverty efforts in Africa, and in 1984 he assembled the charity super-group Band Aid to raise money for famine relief in Ethiopia. Then, Bob went on to organize Live Aid and staged star-studded concert events in England and the U.S. The following year, Geldof produced eight charity mega-concerts, one on every continent, known as Live 8.

Bob Geldof, the man who torpedoed his music career, was later nominated for the Nobel Peace Prize. Now known as Sir Bob Geldof, he was granted an honorary knighthood by Queen Elizabeth II and won the Man of Peace title, awarded to individuals who have made "an outstanding contribution to international social justice and peace." He has devoted much of his life to helping developing countries. In 2002, Bob Geldof was listed as one of the "100 Greatest Britons," despite the fact that he's Irish.

Things do happen for a reason. In the end, he didn't need record labels or radio's help. Geldof's failure as a musician allowed him to redirect his passion and channel it into feeding the world.

Bob Geldof chastising radio execs from the stage—
and killing his singing career

Chapter 25

THE ADVENTURES OF VAN HAGAR

"When you're young and rich and the lead singer of the biggest band in the world, sex is thrown at you."

Sammy Hagar

Sammy Hagar became famous as Van Halen's energetic front man and lead singer. He's the blond California boy who loves fast cars and "can't drive 55." But getting to the top of the rock heap was a long, hard grind. Author Malcom Gladwell believes that it requires 10,000 hours of practice to master your craft. If so, Sammy Hagar is rock music's supreme commander. He was no overnight success; in fact, his road to stardom passed through every beer-soaked, dive bar in America.

In the early '70s, Hagar showed promise as the lead singer for Montrose, the mighty voice behind gems like "Rock Candy," "Bad Motor Scooter" and "Rock The Nation." After Sammy parted ways with Montrose, Capitol Records then threw Hagar a lifeline, signing him to join their label. Sammy busted his ass to

After Hagar left Montrose, he received a $5,000 royalty check. He was broke and living on welfare. But in typical rock star fashion, Sammy spent all of his $5,000 on a Porsche and drove it to pick up his welfare checks.

make it as a solo artist and released eight solo albums before joining Van Halen.

Sammy toured constantly. While on the road, he befriended radio programmers across America. He personally called and visited rock stations wherever he went, and it really paid off. Sammy was one of the first rockers to realize where his bread was buttered. He was a regular guest on radio because he knew how to play the game. While many rock stars are mumbling shoe-gazers in person, Hagar is smart, funny, and likeable. He turned himself inside out to make radio friends, in hopes of getting some airplay. While on tour, Sammy gladly recorded station IDs, invited DJs backstage, posed for a million pictures and signed autographs.

Hagar tried everything to be successful. For years Sammy wore a red jumpsuit onstage and billed himself as the Red Rocker. A nonstarter. He couldn't even get arrested with his own hit song. He wrote and recorded the tune "I've Done Everything For You," and it bombed. Four years later, Rick Springfield recorded the same song and had a top-10 hit. Blessed with one of the greatest rock voices of all time, Sammy couldn't catch a break. While on tour with Kiss in 1977, Hagar's frustration got so bad that he flashed his pecker onstage to show his anger.

Success was elusive and doubt set in. One cold night after a high-energy / low-turnout show, I sat backstage with Sammy. He'd just played a blistering two-hour set for about 1,000 people. Unfortunately, the concert hall held 5,000, so the place felt empty. He was doing all of the right things. But Hagar's career wasn't clicking. Head in his hands and totally spent, Sammy asked, "What's it gonna take, man? I've been doing this for so long. I'm writing good songs, putting out albums, touring my ass off…why aren't people coming to my shows?"

Then, in 1981, Sammy Hagar saw a glimmer of hope. He released an album called *Standing Hampton*, British slang for having an erection. Radio got behind Sammy and played "I'll Fall In Love Again" and "There's Only One Way To Rock." After years of fighting to be heard, Hagar finally earned recognition as a solo artist. His concert tickets became a hot commodity and *Standing Hampton* went platinum, selling more than one million copies. Sammy Hagar's time had finally come.

Whenever his tour came through my town, Sammy would stop by the radio station for an on-air chat. The door was always open. In 1982, during his sold-out tour stop, Hagar came to my office with an idea. He said, "KISW has always been great to me. I'd like to say thanks by wearing your station T-shirt onstage tonight."

"Wow, Sammy, that would be cool." I asked, "So, what do you have in mind?"

"Tonight, the third song in my set will be 'There's Only One Way to Rock.' Before I play it, I'll tear off my shirt and throw it into the crowd. Then, I'll look over to you standing at the side of the stage. Just toss me the KISW shirt and I'll put it on." Seemed simple enough.

It was rare, almost unheard of, for a rock star to endorse a radio station in front of 15,000 fans. But after years of us supporting Sammy, he wanted to pay us back. Later that evening, I showed up at the concert with two shirts in hand, just in case. Hagar's manager, Ed Leffler, and I sat on equipment cases on the side of the stage while Sammy tore through the first two songs. Now came my big moment. Ed and I walked up the stairs and stood behind the curtain, hidden from the crowd. Sammy came over to me and grabbed a towel to mop the sweat. He asked, "Are you ready? Just throw the shirt to me when I look this way."

"Got it, Sammy, I've got the shirt right here," I said, and showed him my hand. The drummer started playing the intro to "There's Only One Way To Rock," and Sammy ran back out to the center of the stage. He was now standing about twenty-five feet away. As the pace picked up, Hagar turned toward me and mouthed the word "now." So I tossed the shirt to him. At that moment, Sammy pulled his sweat-soaked yellow shirt over his head and lobbed it into the crowd. He didn't see the shirt that I'd thrown and looked back toward me, mouthing, "where is it?" Hagar had looked away just long enough to miss the shirt projectile. Luckily, his guitar player saw what happened, and he retrieved our shirt from underneath a speaker monitor. Sammy immediately tore off the sleeves, slipped on our shirt and screamed into the mic, "This is KISW, people! The ooooonly place to rock!" The crowd went crazy as Sammy's band kicked in.

When Van Halen fired David Lee Roth and needed a front man, Hagar was an obvious candidate. In his autobiography, Sammy said he kind of expected Eddie to call. When Hagar did hook up with the Van Halen brothers, he joined a party band that was already in high gear. Sammy learned fast and jumped into the deep end of the pool.

When Hagar did get invited to join Van Halen, his career took a quantum leap. He now sang in stadiums, flew in private jets, sold zillions of albums, lapped the world several times and by his own admission had sex with between fifty and seventy-five women per week. He also enjoyed the fruits of Van Halen's famous party tent that was constructed under the stage. During the concert, Van Halen's roadies would invite groupies into the tent, where they would disrobe and eagerly wait for the band members. Sammy copped to leaving the stage during Eddie Van Halen's long guitar solos and heading down into the tent. There, Hagar found the cure for his recurring case of Restless Dick Syndrome. In his autobiography *Red: My Uncensored Life in Rock*, Sammy admitted, "I fucked everything that walked."

Let me introduce my friend Sky Daniels. He was a popular rock radio DJ and had become good friends with the guys of Van Halen. Sky caught up with the band a few years after Hagar joined Van Halen and shared this memorable experience.

Sky recalls, "Sammy Hagar invited me to drop by their party tent before the show. I've seen craziness happen backstage. And Van Halen had a reputation for being the wildest. So, I was curious to see how much of it was real and how much was legend. I wanted to witness 'The Tent' firsthand. I arrived backstage around 7 p.m., an hour before Van Halen was due to take the stage. I slipped into a restroom and took a Quaalude to help me relax. Then I connected with their road manager, who escorted me through a tunnel of scaffolding into Van Halen's storied tent of sin. They had created a cool, private living room right underneath the stage, totally decked out with couches, rugs, lamps, tables, and plants. It was Van Halen's home away from home."

A few minutes passed before a dozen young girls were led into the tented room, dressed to kill. They were followed by Sammy, the Van Halen brothers and bassist Michael Anthony. Sky recalls, "We sat around on couches while the girls peeled off their clothes and crawled all over the band members. The band would be called to the stage soon, so these ladies were on a mission. Zippers were pulled down as the girls settled in front of their favorite band members. Allegedly." Meanwhile, Sky concentrated on getting wasted with the band and was very successful. An hour later, he was so hammered that he couldn't feel his legs.

Van Halen's road manager came in and announced, "Eddie, Sam, Alex, Michael…you're on in five minutes." The band staggered to their feet and seemed in much better shape than Sky was. Sammy offered, "Why don't you just stay down here and hang out? We'll come back later and pick up where we left off." Sky thought to himself, "Sounds good to me. I can't get off the couch anyway."

Overhead, Sky could hear Van Halen taking the stage about ten feet above him. The crowd roared its approval as Eddie fired out the opening licks to his instrumental masterpiece, "Eruption." The sound was thunderous, and Sky could feel the vibrations in his chest. Still, he was barely conscious and felt himself nodding off. A few minutes later, he heard a voice, far off in the distance. He thought someone had called his name. Sky's eyes rolled back in his head as he listened again. It was Sammy Hagar. "Anybody can sing this next fuckin' song. So, we want to bring out our friend to sing it. Sky Daniels is a DJ here in town. C'mon up here and sing with me, Sky."

What?? Had Sky heard Sammy say his name, or was he hallucinating? Did Sammy say he wants Sky to join Van Halen onstage? Sky sure hoped not, because he was waaay too high. Sky stayed put and closed his eyes. Then he heard Sammy's voice again. "Hey Sky, get up here!"

Daniels remembers, "I felt like I was nailed to the couch. Struggling…to…stay…awake."

"C'mon Sky," Sammy coaxed, "We need you to get up here and sing."

"Whaaa?"

That's when chaos ensued. Two huge bodyguards entered the tent and headed toward Sky, who by now was comatose on the couch. The large men shoved their hands under his armpits and lifted Sky up in one motion. Before he realized what hit him, the security guys dragged Daniels out of the tent and toward the stairs leading up to the stage. Sky's feet churned in the air, trying to get traction, like in a Roadrunner cartoon. Van Halen's goons pushed him up the final few steps to the stage. Then…KABBONNG! Sky slammed his head on a metal girder, suspended horizontally at eye level. "The guys in Van Halen are kinda short", Sky relates, "So they had no trouble walking under that cross beam. But I'm 6-5 and that bar caught me flush in the forehead. It felt like Mike Tyson punched me between the eyes. Not only was I whacked out of my mind, now I've got a concussion!"

When Eddie Van Halen saw Sky arrive on the side of the stage, he put down his guitar and walked over to play the organ. Sky recalls, "Eddie was on the keyboards and started playing the intro to their song 'Jump.'" Sammy ran over and started pulling Sky on stage by his shirt. The DJ's knees wobbled as Hagar dragged Daniels all over the stage by his elbow. Eddie kept playing the organ intro to "Jump" as Sammy ran the wasted jock up and down the riser platforms. Sky admits that he was about to pass out when Hagar stopped, handed him a wireless microphone, and yelled, "Alright Sky, *you* sing."

"*Me* sing? First of all, I can't sing. Second of all, I am out of breath and too high to remember the words. There's just no way. Eddie Van Halen had finished the 'Jump' intro and was waving for me to sing the first verse. So, I held the mic to my mouth and groggily sputtered the words 'guitar solo.' It was all I could think of. Eddie was all the way across the stage. He looked at me and shrugged as if to say, 'Huh?' The nearest guitar was twenty feet away." Sammy was now standing at the center of the stage, also sans guitar. In other words, there would be no guitar solo. "I dropped the mic," says Sky, "and stumbled off the stage." So much for his fifteen seconds of fame. Epic fail.

After performing for decades, Sammy Hagar finally hit the mother lode. But he didn't make his fortune just in music.

Hagar really cashed in when he sold his Cabo Wabo Tequila company for more than $100 million.

If there's one guy who deserves that kind of success, it's Sammy Hagar.

Before: The early days with Sammy Hagar

After: With Van Halen

Chapter 26

I SEE DEAD
(VILLAGE) PEOPLE

"I feel the same way about disco as I do about herpes."

Hunter S. Thompson

Radio stations were fiercely competitive in the 1980s. KISW battled several stations for Seattle's rock crown, including an upstart known simply as "The X." We tried to clobber each other at every turn. Most of the time, listeners had no idea of the devious schemes that competing stations plotted to sabotage one another. It was not uncommon for station A to set up its van in a parking lot to broadcast music from the sound system. Meanwhile, station B would sabotage station A with a louder sound system and simply drown them out.

In September of 1989, I got wind that The X was planning a big Halloween party. Their DJs hinted that the band was a huge star and "very scary." My station had no time to assemble our own Halloween show. So my first thought was, "How can we undermine theirs?" A few days later, The X started airing commercials for their party, instructing listeners to "Stay tuned for the big announcement of our spooky Halloween party, featuring a very scary band." We could only guess which big, scary artist was headlining the party. Because the X was a rock station, I expected them to showcase a super-statar like Ozzy Osbourne, the Prince of Darkness. Or maybe Alice Cooper, who was famous for albums like *Welcome To My Nightmare*. At least that would be quirky and cool.

As a rock station, KISW saw disco as plastic music for shallow people. It was the antithesis of genuine, passionate rock. Discos were for phonies, John Travolta wannabes in white suits and gold chains. KISW had such disdain for that music that we blew up disco songs on the air. We were inspired by a Chicago DJ named Steve Dahl who encouraged his fans to bring vinyl disco albums to a White Sox game. He staged an on-field demolition and used dynamite to literally explode a pile of records between games of a doubleheader. Shards of vinyl records flew hundreds of feet in the air. The blast caused so much damage to the field at Comiskey Park that umpires cancelled the second game and the White Sox forfeited.

KISW's evening jock, Steve Slaton, made the same impact - but he took a safer approach. He used sound effects to blow up disco songs on the air. Slaton started by bombing the worst offenders: Donna Summer, the Bee Gees, Kool & the Gang and KC and the Sunshine Band. But Steve's favorite target was the Village People. What began as a one-off bit really struck a nerve with our listeners—and took off. Soon, Slaton was blowing up a different disco song every night, to the delight of rock fans. During the height of "Disco Destruction" mania, Steve took the stage at a Cheap Trick concert and recruited 9,000 fans, en masse, to join KISW's Rock & Roll Air Force. I stood near the stage next to Cheap Trick's manager and watched in awe as the crowd raised their right hands in unison and promised to "wipe out the scourge of disco in our lifetime."

Whenever Slaton demolished a song like "YMCA," he would start playing the record and then manually

slip the turntable into a neutral gear, which disengaged the motor. Without power, the song s-l-o-w-s down. Meanwhile he had loaded up sound effects of heavy mortar fire. When Steve started pressing buttons, the song was soon overwhelmed by a cacophony of bombs, machine guns and rocket launchers. He threw the works at it. As the disco song writhed in its death throes, Slaton lined up his kill shot, and fired a blast that finally stopped the tune cold...putting an end to its suffering.

Finally, The X announced their show details. They were hosting a Halloween party at Union Station, a converted landmark in downtown Seattle. Tickets were $10 per person. And the "scary" band they hired was...the Village People. Say what? The Village People? Why would a rock station feature a disco band? Didn't they know that rock fans *hated* disco? If The X thought that bringing in the Village People was clever, their listeners didn't get the joke. Rock fans wouldn't pay a dime to see a Village People show. This Halloween party was going to bomb. But it wasn't enough for The X's show to face-plant. We set out to make them look even more ridiculous.

Over the next few days, we tracked the ticket sales for The X's concert. Despite a heavy promotional push, the Halloween party was tanking. Union Station held 1,100 people. But as of twenty-four hours before the show, Ticketmaster had only sold 100 tickets. A disaster.

I came to work on October 31st and was met by our morning DJ, Bob Rivers. He said, "Boss, I've got a great idea to sabotage The X's Halloween party tonight. Ticket sales suck, and they are going to lose their ass on this show. This will really humiliate them."

"Great, let's hear it," I replied, eager to stick it to our nemesis.

Rivers mischievously laid out his plan. "Right across from Union Station is a big wino park that's usually filled with drunks who sleep on the benches. The weather forecast is for a cold rain tonight, and these guys will want to stay dry. So, let's buy 100 tickets to The X's Halloween party and give them to the winos! They can be our special guests at the party!"

It was devious. It was politically incorrect. It was brilliant. For the bargain rate of $1,000, we could turn The X's Halloween party into a nightmare. It was the perfect sting operation that would totally demoralize our biggest competitor. The X would suspect we were behind it, but they couldn't prove anything. So, our business manager cut a $1,000 check to Ticketmaster, and Rivers took off to buy 100 tickets. Meanwhile, we assembled a team of volunteers to help distribute party tickets to the winos.

After the sun went down, five of us dressed in dark clothes and packed into one car. Fifteen minutes later, we drove past the wino park and scoped out the area. As forecast, it was a cold, rainy evening. We parked about two blocks from Union Station and walked to the wino park from there. As we approached, dozens of drunks, derelicts, and hobos were settling in for a long cold night on the park benches. By the light of the streetlamps, we could see them taking shelter under dirty tarps and wet blankets.

Across from the park, a mere 100 yards away, all of the lights shone brightly at Union Station. The streets were empty and so was The X's ticket line. Not a soul in sight. So being good Samaritans, we set out to help liven up their event. Our team of five fanned out across the park, each with twenty party tickets in our pockets. I approached the first group of winos, and the stench was overwhelming—a blend of cheap wine, body odor and piss. Undeterred, I walked up to the bums and smiled, "Hi guys, I've got some Halloween treats you might like," and held out the tickets. "How would you like to go to a Halloween party tonight, right across the street?" (as I pointed to Union Station). That got their attention, so I pressed on, "It's warm and dry inside, with food, beer, music and hot women. I've got free tickets for everyone."

Now they were all ears. "Who wants to go to the Halloween party?" The winos flashed toothless grins and nodded eagerly. So, I placed tickets in twenty grimy hands and headed back to connect with my fellow ticket ninjas. Within a half hour, we had handed out all 100 tickets. What followed was like a scene from *Night of the Living Dead*. It was an amazing sight to watch 100 tattered winos staggering toward Union Station. We watched from the shadows as an army of slow-moving drunks lurched toward the Halloween event, arms outstretched and hands clutching their party tickets. Great costumes, guys. Everybody dressed as a hobo! If only I had a video camera.

I can only imagine what happened as the stinking band of wet zombies approached the front door of Union Station. The winos had tickets, so legally they had the right to enter the party. The doorman had no choice but to admit the tattered mob. Now, with only 100 legit guests inside the party, our smelly friends accounted for *half* of the crowd. It wouldn't take long before the paying guests got a whiff of the new arrivals and headed for the nearest exit.

On this night, the Village People played to a small, but receptive audience. Hell, the 100 bums were just happy to be warm and dry. And KISW was happy to pull off another coup and piss off our competitor.

Sing it with me…

Young man, there's a place you can go.
I said, young man, when you're short on your dough.
You can stay there, and I'm sure you will find,
Many ways to have a good time…at the Y-M-C-A.

HOW DID YOU HEAR ABOUT THE YMCA	
(Please check one)	
____ Television	____ Online
____ Radio	____ Drove By
____ Ad in paper	____ Family/Friend
____ Postcard	____ Other ✗ Village
____ Return Member	____ Insurance People
____ Email	____ Billboard

Chapter 27

HEART WAS THE WALRUS

> "I'm a little bit more unusual,
> so I consider myself as the black sheep."
>
> **Ann Wilson**

Let me first say that I'm a big fan of the band Heart. Ann Wilson is unquestionably one of the greatest rock singers of all time. Maybe the best. But after this incident, Ann wasn't a big fan of Beau Phillips.

Seattle is the hometown of Jimi Hendrix, Pearl Jam, Nirvana, Soundgarden, Alice in Chains and others. But Heart's Ann and Nancy Wilson are the pride and joy of the Emerald City. They are local heroes, and deservedly so. The Wilson sisters have been great ambassadors for Seattle, and the town is unabashedly proud of their Rock and Roll Hall of Fame inductees. Inspired by the Beatles, the sisters sang together at an early age. Ann, the older Wilson sister, is the powerhouse voice behind "Magic Man," "Crazy On You" and "Barracuda." Nancy is Heart's virtuoso guitarist and backup singer. Nancy is a slim blonde and a natural beauty. Ann is dark-haired and attractive, but hardly slim.

As the program director of Seattle's top rock station, I got to know and like the members of Heart. Over the years, we'd bump into one another at local concerts, events, and appearances. Sometimes, Nancy and her (then) husband Cameron Crowe would drop by my station to grab some new CDs. I was also friendly with their manager, Ken Kinnear, and even bought my home from Heart's producer and friend, Mike Flicker.

For many years, Heart released new albums on Valentine's Day. And on those special days, it became a tradition for the Wilson sisters to visit our studios and deliver their latest album in person. The sisters would hang out with the DJ on-air, play a few songs from their new album, and take calls from listeners. Heart's Valentine's Day visits were always a love fest as fans celebrated the beloved Wilson sisters.

But there was no love shared on this Valentine's Day.

It was February 14, 1980. I was the jock on duty when Ann and Nancy stopped by to present their new album, *Bebe Le Strange*. The album cover features a black-and-white head shot of Ann and Nancy Wilson, looking sexy with permed hair. The sisters are sitting side by side and looking directly into the camera.

Heart's visit began as it usually did, as a celebration. We'd received an advance copy of *Bebe Le Strange* and had been playing cuts from it for a few days. To Seattle rock fans, hearing a new Heart album on the radio was special, like unwrapping a present. So, I was looking forward to having the Wilson sisters come by the station on Valentine's Day to talk about their new record.

Our staff greeted Ann and Nancy Wilson in the lobby, and they shook hands with everyone and graciously posed for pictures. After a bit of mingling, the ladies from Heart were escorted down the hallway to our on-air studio. I saw the heavy control room door swing open, and there stood Seattle's most famous sisters.

I understand that celebrity photos are commonly airbrushed. But the Ann Wilson standing before me looked nothing like the woman on the *Bebe Le Strange* cover. Where was the sultry brunette with the come hither look? No camera trickery could hide the fact that Ann had put on weight. It's no secret that Ann has struggled with her weight over the years, and she'd been widely ridiculed by the media. I'm sure that Ann heard the jabs and was hurt by the nagging criticism. While she tried valiantly to lose weight, the truth is that Ann never had the svelte figure expected of a female rock star. She tried camouflaging herself in billowing black outfits, exercised, and even had lap band surgery to curb her appetite. But nothing worked, and Ann still cast a large shadow.

Back to our studio on Valentine's Day. Ann and Nancy were excited to talk about their new album. While they do a million interviews, this was their Seattle homecoming—a chance to premiere *Bebe Le Strange* to their legions of local fans. The Wilson sisters eagerly settled in behind guest microphones and slipped on their headphones. It was all downhill from there.

The Heart interview was going well until Ann suggested we play a track from *Bebe LeStrange*. So, I pulled out the vinyl disc from the album cover and set the cover aside. I set the needle down "Even It Up." The girls introduced it, thanking Tower of Power's horn section for giving the song a brassy punch. While the tune was playing, I turned down the volume in the studio so we could chat while the mics were off. Ann remarked, "We really jammed to get the record released by Valentine's Day. So, I haven't even seen the final album cover artwork yet. We used the renowned photographer Annie Leibovitz, so I'm really excited to see how it came out." Ann extended her hand toward me and asked, "Can I take a look at the album jacket?"

I knew that our copy of *Bebe Le Strange* had only been in the on-air studio for a few days. But it didn't take long for

In 1980, radio stations played vinyl records. While the songs played, DJs would often read the album covers and sometimes write snide remarks, draw smiley faces or add moustaches. At KISW, our jocks elevated album cover graffiti to an art form. They wrote hilarious comments on albums, creating ongoing private jokes. Because the covers were hidden inside our studio, artists never saw the snarky comments we'd scribble on their record sleeves. Over the years, some LP jackets had ongoing dialogues that filled the entire cover. We even created a Hall of Fame for the funniest album cover graffiti.

our DJs to deface album covers. When Ann asked to see the LP jacket, I cringed. Something told me not to show it to her.

Before I handed the album cover to Ann, the song ended, and I got a brief respite. Back on the air again, we resumed our interview, and I opened the phone lines to let callers chat with Heart. Secretly, I was hoping to distract Ann so she'd forget all about the cover. With the ladies occupied for the moment, I wanted to get a good look at the jacket. I felt it leaning against my right leg. While Ann excitedly told fans about Heart's tour plans, I reached down to steal a peek at our only copy of *Bebe Le Strange.* Damn! My worst fears were confirmed when I saw four words scribbled on the album cover. There was only one comment, but it was hurtful. Someone had drawn a cartoon bubble coming from Ann's mouth with the words "I Am The Walrus." I knew that if Ann saw the defaced cover she would be devastated.

After hanging up with the last caller, Nancy suggested, "Why don't we play another song from *Bebe Le Strange*?"

"Good idea," I agreed, again happy the jacket would be forgotten. I cued up the title track, and pressed play. Feeling the tension, I started babbling, trying to buy some time. This time, Ann looked directly at me, annoyed, and said, "Would you hand me the album cover?"

The graffiti was extremely rude. Funny, but rude. Criticizing Ann's weight really twisted the knife in a woman who'd battled her weight publicly. Worse yet, Ann was an avid Beatles fan. So I knew the "walrus" reference would add insult to injury. I was mortified, and my mind was racing, thinking of ways to avoid showing the album cover to Ann. I considered yelling, "Fire!" Or pretending that I'd passed out. If there was any way to slither under the door and disappear, I would have tried. But we were alone in the studio, sitting three feet apart. I was doomed.

"It's probably best if you get a copy from your record label, Ann," I balked, starting to sweat. "This is our only copy and it gets beaten up and scribbled on."

She sloughed off my objections, "I don't mind. I'd still like to see it, please."

My stomach churned as I handed over the *Bebe Le Strange* cover. I watched Ann's eyes as she took her first look at Heart's latest creation. She stared at the grafitti, and the color drained from her face. I saw the hurt in her eyes. While I didn't write the "I Am The Walrus" gag, it didn't matter. I was there, representing the station. So, I faced the music.

There was nothing I could say to take back those four stinging words. No words would wipe that image out of Ann's mind. No apology would excuse the pain that it caused her. No matter what I said or did, this was going to end badly. "I'm sorry, Ann," I offered. "The jocks here are a bunch of idiots who make fun of everyone. Please don't take it personally."

Ann, the more vocal Wilson sister, immediately went silent. I expected a Valentine's Day massacre. But she was too stunned and hurt to tell me off. As the air left the room, Nancy draped her arm around Ann's shoulder to comfort her big sister. Clearly, our visit was over. The women hastily gathered their belongings and left without a word.

When the song ended, I turned on the mic and had to fake it. "That was the title song to *Bebe Le Strange*. Ann and Nancy had to leave. But we thank them for spending Valentine's Day with us." By then, the Wilson sisters had beat a hasty retreat to the parking lot and were long gone.

It took years for me to mend the relationship with Heart. But they say time heals all wounds. So, I tested that theory in the early '90s, when I invited Ann Wilson to dinner. Her assistant, Kelly Curtis (now Pearl Jam's manager), helped me put it together and asked Ann on my behalf. She graciously accepted, and I took that as a good sign. We met at a popular waterfront restaurant in Seattle, drawing stares throughout our meal. We kept the conversation light and easy. While I kept waiting for her to drop a bomb, she never did. Ann and I spent two pleasant hours talking about everything from Led Zeppelin to life on the road to our kids. I felt a bit lighter when we called it a night.

Thankfully, there was no mention of the "walrus incident... until now.

Chapter 28

RISING STARS AND
ONE-HIT WONDERS

"In the future, everyone will be famous
for fifteen minutes."

Andy Warhol

Radio stations and record companies have a symbiotic relationship. They could not exist without each other, and they wash each other's backs, so to speak. Radio stations need the music that record labels provide. It's their currency to attract listeners and advertisers. Record labels need radio airplay to promote their artists to music buyers. It's a quid pro quo arrangement that somehow works.

Each week, radio music directors talk with representatives from record labels to discuss their latest song releases. The label pleads its case, hoping to earn a cherished slot on the station's playlist. But the vast majority of new songs never see the light of day on radio. As a result, less than 1 percent of album releases are financially successful. So, a lot of pressure is put on labels to get airplay, or "spins," on popular stations.

With so much on the line, record labels go to great lengths to gain radio's favor. They're willing to do almost anything to get their songs played. During radio's heyday, record companies fawned over radio programmers and showered them with attention, favors and—if necessary—cash.

Of course, payola was illegal. Record companies are not allowed to "pay for play" without disclosing that money changed hands. But that didn't stop some program directors from taking bribes from labels under the table. Many record company execs would ask me, "What would it take to get you to play this song?" The question was so vague and open-ended that I didn't know how to respond. Or I was too stupid to realize they were offering to buy my cooperation. While he was governor of New York (and before he became known as "client 9") Eliot Spitzer uncovered a payola scandal and prosecuted the offenders to the hilt. That didn't stop record labels from paying off program directors. They just got more creative.

The top echelon of rock radio stations, fewer than twenty of us, often determined the fate of new bands. It was a responsibility that we rock programmers took seriously. Once a band started to get traction, stations would bring them to town for "low dough" Rising Star-type shows. For a few bucks, our listeners could discover a star on the rise.

Label reps would routinely camp out in station lobbies for hours, waiting for their turn to pitch new songs. But it was time well spent, because popular stations had control over artists' careers. Station PDs were the gatekeepers who decided which bands would be heard, and which bands would not. Like King Solomon, radio execs had ultimate power whether to give artists a thumbs up or thumbs down. Would the band have a music career? Or would they be sent back to the drawing board, or more often into oblivion?

KISW was particularly friendly to new artists. When we heard a band that struck a nerve, we'd rally behind them.

Our decisions were based on gut instinct. Choosing songs was art, not science. Our listeners trusted our judgment to help them discover new bands and songs. Our DJs would talk artists up and encourage listeners to buy tickets to our Rising Star concerts, showcases that earned a national reputation for launching careers.

Rising Star concerts were the essence of music discovery. They let fans experience superstars on their way to the top. We created that special moment, that feeling in the pit of your stomach when the lights go down and you see an artist for the first time…that brief pause of anticipation before the stage comes alive with lights and the adrenaline makes your heart leap.

Producing a Rising Star show required cooperation from my station, the band, managers, the record label, the concert promoter, record stores and the venue. None of us made money on these shows. We recognized the benefit of giving bands a boost and agreed to contribute our time and effort to showcasing bands. Then, if an artist truly became a star, as many did, we'd already established a relationship and would build on that success.

To pull off a Rising Star show also required the band to perform for free. It was an investment in their career. Record labels paid the band's travel expenses, and concert promoters waived their fee and took no profit. My radio station promoted the Rising Star concerts and encouraged listeners to check out a band destined for greatness.

Choosing a Rising Star band was a crapshoot. Sometimes, bands showed promise from day one, clearly on their way to the top. Other times, the artists needed more seasoning. Some sounded great on vinyl, but put on a boring live show. Then there were the groups that got lucky once, but it ended there. Such was the story of Tommy Tutone, the band behind "867-5309/Jenny." Lead singer Tommy Heath told WGN in Chicago, "867-5309 was the phone number of a girl I knew. As a joke, I wrote it on a bathroom wall in a motel where we were staying."

The song became a hit, but it was also a huge nuisance for those with that phone number. Complaints were lodged across the country from people who were besieged with prank callers who jokingly responded to the song's refrain, "for a good time, call." Our Rising Star concert with Tommy Tutone was a sellout. But the band's success was short-lived. After seeing them perform "867-5309," fans left and soon forgot about Tommy Tutone. The band was reduced to a trivia question and then banished to the island of one-hit wonders.

Then there were the flat-out failures. I once got a call from Epic Records wanting to do a Rising Star show featuring their hot new band, the Fabulous Poodles. After getting buried in hype, I agreed to support their show, but it was a disaster. The name alone should have scared me away. The Fab Poos were flamboyant—dressed in pink—and laughably bad. The crowd made a beeline for the exit after the first song. After dropping a turd onstage, the poodles tucked their tails between their legs and were never heard from again.

On the other hand, Toto was a huge band in the '80s after getting their start at a KISW Rising Star concert. Our audience loved their first hit, "Hold The Line." Before Toto went on to record elevator music like "Africa" and "Rosanna," they were a rock band. Named after the dog in the *Wizard of Oz*, Toto was composed of elite session musicians. Their lead singer, Bobby Kimball, had a terrific voice. But he lacked the physique of a prototypical rock singer. Front men like Mick Jagger, Steve Tyler and David Lee Roth were long and lean, in tremendous condition. Bobby was short and stocky.

When Toto played our Rising Star show, tickets were priced at just $2 and sold out immediately. Their musicianship was impressive, and the band played a scorching set. About midway through the concert, Bobby Kimball took a leap of faith and jumped off the stage so he could work the crowd. With mic in hand, he stood among the fans and sang a few lines. Then, during the guitar solo, Kimball scrambled back toward the stage. He had about fifteen seconds before the next verse and took a running jump at the four-foot stage. Bobby came up well short and fell backward. He got up, smiled sheepishly and tried again. This time it was even worse. Kimball couldn't swing his right leg high enough, and he slid back once again. By now, people were starting to snicker. It was too late to get up to the mic in time, so Bobby finished the song right where he stood. After the lights went down, two roadies rolled him back up. I doubt that Bobby Kimball ever ventured into the crowd again.

Rising Star shows gave aspiring bands a jump start. We gave them the opportunity to impress fans, and we were proud to play a part. Over the years, KISW introduced fans to many stars who truly *did* rise, including Sammy Hagar, Elvis Costello, Talking Heads, Robert Palmer, Blondie, Pat Benatar and a kid from Sayreville, New Jersey named Jon Bongiovi...

Chapter 29

INTRODUCING
JON BONGIOVI

"Success is falling nine times—and getting up ten."

Jon Bon Jovi

The year was 1982. John Lassman was the nineteen-year-old promotion director for WAPP-FM, aka "the Apple." For a brief time, it was the number-one radio station in New York City. The station played no commercials for the entire summer and vaulted from worst to first. The Apple stayed on top of the ratings heap...until they had to start playing commercials. Then, the bottom fell out, and the station lost its mojo.

During WAPP's brief heyday, Miller Beer asked the station to be its promotional partner for a "Homegrown" album. Miller wanted to produce a compilation album that featured the best songs by local bands from the New York area. Lassman explains, "Our role was to collect tapes from local bands, screen the entries, and help decide which bands and songs would make it onto the Homegrown record. The artist who delivered the best song would win an album deal with Atlantic Records."

The entry deadline for submitting demo tapes for the Homegrown album was on a Friday at 5 p.m. Lassman recalls, "Around 4:59 p.m., I got a call from the Apple's receptionist asking me to come to the lobby. As I walked into the room, I was approached by a guy with long, permed hair. He stuck out his hand and introduced himself: 'Hi, I'm Jon Bongiovi.'

He looked to be about my age and was very direct. Jon looked me straight in the eye and explained, 'I have a song for your Homegrown album. Sorry for getting here at the last minute. But I wanted to deliver my demo in person, so I drove up from New Jersey.' "

Lassman eagerly continues, "I remember that Jon handed me a black cassette with just one song on it, called 'Runaway.' He'd scribbled down his name and work phone number, which was for a pizza joint he worked at in New Jersey. I threw Jon's demo tape into the box along with the other hopeful bands and got ready to head out for the weekend. I'm not sure why, but something told me to fish out Bongiovi's black cassette and give it a listen."

Lassman sat back in his office chair, popped in the cassette, and pressed play. "I immediately noticed the professional sound quality. It stood out. Not something recorded in a garage. Over the weekend, I listened to 'Runaway' again and couldn't believe what I was hearing from a Jersey bar band. To my ears, it sounded like a rock radio hit. The next Monday, I called Jon Bongiovi and told him, 'Yours was the last demo submitted. But it was worth waiting for. I think "Runaway" is sure to be a finalist on Miller Beer's Homegrown album. Plus, WAPP is going to play your song in rotation, along with Led Zeppelin et. al.' "

Bongiovi was psyched by Lassman's encouragement and proudly admitted, "My cousin is one of the owners of the Power Station recording studio in Manhattan. I help him clean up and he lets me record demos there."

Lassman recalls "The WAPP team collected and listened to more than 300 tapes from local bands. Then we met with the Miller Beer guys to choose the best songs for the Homegrown album. In our opinion, 'Runaway' was the best tune we'd heard. But, Jon Bongiovi faced heavy competition from two Long Island bands, Zebra and Twisted Sister. Those looked like the top three contenders for the record deal." Not a bad local crop.

When the winner was announced, "Runaway" was named the best song and won the contract with Atlantic Records. But as it turned out, Jon turned it down. After hearing "Runaway" on WAPP, Mercury Records swooped in to offer Bongiovi a record deal. So, the Atlantic contract was awarded to Zebra. Both Zebra and Dee Snider's Twisted Sister went on to enjoy national success, and their debut albums were certified gold. Jon Bongiovi's first record sold more than one million copies and earned platinum status.

When Miller Beer's Homegrown album was released, my friend at WAPP sent me a copy. We got wind of the buzz for Bongiovi's "Runaway" and started playing the song on KISW. Listeners reacted immediately. The more that we played "Runaway," the more requests we got for it. After a few weeks, it was clear that Jon Bongiovi was on his way.

As interest was heating up across the country, Mercury suggested that Jon shorten and Americanize the band's name to simply Bon Jovi. Word about "Runaway" was spreading like wildfire as radio programmers jumped on Jon's song and were telling their friends. I called John Bauer, the local concert promoter, and told him about Bon Jovi. KISW had established a wonderful partnership with Bauer, and we'd collaborated on more than thirty-five Rising Star concerts. When KISW gave a band our Rising Star seal of approval, people wanted to be there.

By 1983, radio stations around the country were booking Bon Jovi concerts in their towns, so Mercury Records sent Jon and his bandmates on tour. My station was one of the earliest stations to get behind the band, and our Rising Star concert was one of Jon's first shows outside of New Jersey.

I have to give credit to the guys in Queensrÿche. They were kids from the Seattle suburbs who were looking for a break. They were passionate about their band and occasionally called to ask about opportunities to be the opening act at one of our shows. I liked their enthusiasm and was waiting for the right time to give them a chance.

KISW teased that there was a big announcement coming. The following morning, Jon Bon Jovi called our station to announce the show himself. He gave out the concert details and ticket info. Then, Jon ended with a flourish by announcing that the opening band would be a local group called Queensrÿche.

I called Scott Rockenfeld from Queensrÿche and invited his band to open for Bon Jovi. He screamed with excitement. Then I asked, "What's the most people that Queensrÿche has played for"?

Slight pause. "About 200."

I hesitated and then reminded him, "There will be 3,000 people in the Paramount for this concert. Can you guys handle it?"

"Just give us the chance," he answered, without missing a beat.

Two weeks later, the big night arrived. Queensrÿche took the stage and was impressive. They were clearly green and kept looking at each other. But singer Geoff Tate's operatic voice seethed with pure rock passion.

When Bon Jovi followed, there was a dramatic jump in class and professionalism. There was no doubt that we were watching a star in the making. Jon's set was unpolished, but powerful. When he grabbed the mic, Bon Jovi owned the stage. From the very beginning, he had a commanding presence. Afterward, I went back to meet Jon backstage. Wearing a long fur coat, he looked the part and had the undeniable aura of a rock star.

Lassman had the same impression of the future star. "When I met Jon Bongiovi, he was a very polite kid. But even then you could feel his intensity. He didn't want to settle, which explains the first-class demo he recorded at the Power Station. Word has it that Jon was the first artist to take his laptop on the road and check how many stations were playing his song. If he spotted declines in airplay anywhere, he would grill the label's promotion team, demanding to know the reason why. Jon was more than the band leader. He acted like the CEO, with a very demanding style and a good sense of the music business."

To date, Bon Jovi has sold more than 130 million records worldwide and performed more than 2,700 concerts in 50 countries. He is also among the most humanitarian rock artists. *Forbes* magazine ranks Jon Bon Jovi the number-one celebrity in terms of translating his fame into goodwill. He pours his time and his name into worthy causes via his JBJ Soul Foundation.

A very young Queensrÿche after their debut

With Jon Bon Jovi right after his Rising Star concert

Hanging out with Jon (center) and his bandmates

Chapter 30

THANKSGIVING
WITH THE BENATARS

"Most chick singers say 'if you hurt me, I'll die.'
I say, 'if you hurt me, I'll kick your ass.' "

Pat Benatar

In 1979, most radio stations were still playing vinyl records. On very rare occasions, a record label rep would bring in a "test pressing," which looked like a regular twelve-inch record, but was a lot thicker and stiffer. Test pressings were made of acetate and were produced in very small quantities. The fragile discs would shatter like dinner plates if they were dropped. Unlike vinyl albums, test pressings were brittle and could only be played a few times before the audio quality degraded. Record labels only went to the expense of producing acetate copies for artists they really believed in. Before an album was released, labels would produce a few test pressings and play them for influential people. The discs would last long enough to gauge reaction, then were discarded.

That summer, I got a call from my label rep from Chrysalis Records. "I know that your station loves to discover new artists. You were the first to play Billy Idol's first hit 'White Wedding.' Well, I've got another artist that you've got to hear. Her name is Pat Benatar. She's a real rock singer who's perfect for your station."

"Yeah, right," I said. "Never heard that line before." However, I couldn't remember the last time I'd heard a powerful female rock singer. Back then, rock singers were dudes with big hair and spandex. So, I was intrigued to hear this hot new singer.

The Chrysalis rep pressed on, "Can I come by tomorrow and play Pat's song for you? Trust me, you'll like it."

The next morning, our label rep came up to my office and removed the test pressing from its protective sleeve. He gently placed the acetate disc on my turntable, rested the needle on the outside groove and said, "This is Pat Benatar, and the song is called 'Heartbreaker.' "

The song charges right out of the chute with a driving beat. First came the pounding drums, followed by the bass. Then the guitar kicks in, and Pat Benatar snarls...

"Your love is like a tidal wave, spinning over my head.
Drownin' me in your promises, better left unsaid."

Wow. I liked "Heartbreaker" immediately. Unlike soft rock female singers like Stevie Nicks and Carly Simon, Pat Benatar sang with raw power. She had an attitude, an edge that didn't sound like anything else on our station. Then, she took it up a notch.

"You're a heartbreaker, dream maker, love taker
Don't you mess around with me."

Once the guitar solo kicked in, I was sold. I picked up the phone and called Steve Slaton, our music director, and asked him to join us. As he walked in, Benatar's guitarist unleashed a solo that wrapped around Pat's voice, and "Heartbreaker" built to a peak. Slaton and I looked at each other in disbelief. We knew that the Chrysalis rep was right. "Heartbreaker" was a perfect fit for our station.

When the song ended, the wheels were turning in my head. I knew I'd just heard something special and asked the label rep, "How many other stations have heard this?"

"None," he answered. "You're my first stop."

I jumped in, "Great. We'll take this test pressing and put 'Heartbreaker' on the air today, right now." I thought the Chrysalis rep would wet himself. This never happened. Big radio stations never put a brand new artist in hot rotation without a rep's haggling and begging. But here was a respected rock station offering to give Pat Benatar the star treatment on day one. We were offering to play Chrysalis's newbie artist alongside Led Zeppelin, Pink Floyd and the Stones.

"But, I'm only supposed to play the song for people and get opinions," he said. "The album isn't even available in stores yet."

I looked at the label rep and gave him the good news: "Look, I love this song. She has a huge voice and a tremendous future. We want to play the hell out of "Heartbreaker" and help you make Pat Benatar a star." His eyes lit up.

"But here's the deal," I said. "You've got to leave the test pressing here. We've got to be the *only* station in town playing the song. So, you can't bring this acetate to any other stations. I want to play it exclusively, or we don't play it at all."

"Oh, come on man," the rep griped. "You're putting me in a tough spot. Of course, we'd love to have your station's support. But I can't give you an exclusive."

I suggested that he call his boss, the VP of promotion for Chrysalis Records in Los Angeles. "Tell him that KISW is ready to go all-in with Pat Benatar. But we need a two-week head start over everyone else."

The Chrysalis rep left my office to call his boss. He returned a few minutes later with a pained look on his face. "My boss wants to talk with you," he said.

I picked up the phone and put the L.A. boss on the speakerphone. He laid out all of the reasons why Chrysalis didn't want to give my station an exclusive window for Pat Benatar. In fairness, he had some good points, starting with, "We haven't even manufactured or shipped her album yet. It won't be available in stores for two weeks."

"So, KISW will start playing Benatar right now. Let my listeners get used to 'Heartbreaker.' Then, in two weeks, people will be hungry to buy it."

Mr. Chrysalis responded, "We just wanted to drum up interest in 'Heartbreaker.' We're not quite ready to release it for airplay yet. We just produced three test pressings. You've got one of them."

"I understand," I sympathized. Not wanting to take no for an answer, I countered with, "Let me ask you something. How many other radio stations have stepped up and offered to jam your new artist in hot rotation…right out of the blocks?"

The Chrysalis rep volleyed back with, "You'd be the first station in the country to play Pat Benatar. Honestly, we'd rather have you wait until we've got more stations on board so we can build momentum. But if you really want to run with 'Heartbreaker,' I'll keep it from other stations and give you an exclusive shot for two weeks."

With that news, I turned Slaton loose with the test pressing and instructed him to save a master copy of "Heartbreaker," as a backup. We couldn't play the acetate disc on-air because the fidelity would deteriorate after a few plays. So, he recorded "Heartbreaker" onto a "cart," which resembled an 8-track cartridge. For two weeks, KISW played "Heartbreaker" every few hours. The more we played "Heartbreaker," the more calls we got from listeners requesting it. We talked up Pat Benatar as a tough rock chick with a voice that had urgency. She had an angst that made you believe that some guy had screwed her over—and now he was gonna pay. Benatar's momentum was starting to pound like jungle drums in the distance. And the drums kept getting louder. So I went to work on getting Pat to headline at our next Rising Star concert.

A few months passed and the rest of America discovered Pat Benatar as well. "Heartbreaker" raced up the charts while the album *In The Heat of The Night* went multi-platinum. Pat called our station to thank us for being early believers, and she announced her Rising Star concert in Seattle. It would be the day before Thanksgiving, and when tickets sold out almost immediately, rock fans confirmed our instincts. If Pat Benatar could perform as well as she sounded in a recording studio, this was going to be a helluva show.

I was the DJ on duty on the afternoon of Pat Benatar's Rising Star concert. Her Chrysalis Records rep called to say that Pat and her guitarist (and future husband) Neil Giraldo wanted to stop by the station before their show. "Absolutely!" I said and invited them to join me in the studio.

Ten minutes later, the control room door swung open and there stood Pat Benatar. In person, the powerhouse singer with the mezzo-soprano voice is petite, maybe five feet tall. Dressed in tight black leather pants and a striped shirt, Pat demurely stood behind Giraldo. The Chrysalis Records rep was right behind her, carrying a fully cooked turkey with all the trimmings. Pat came around the console to shake my hand, explaining, "We wanted to say thanks for all you've done by bringing you a Thanksgiving feast."

"You're welcome, we love your album, Pat. It's burning up our request lines and tonight's show should be packed. Now please sit down and help me eat this turkey while you talk to some listeners." The rep set down the bird while Pat and Neil settled in behind our guest microphones. She had taken the rock world by storm. Now, it was time to introduce Pat Benatar to her fans.

As Pat chatted with listeners on the air, I realized that we didn't have any knives or utensils at the radio station. Maybe small plastic knives. But nothing that would carve a turkey. So, with no silverware, we used our hands to tear off chunks of meat and made toasts with soda in plastic cups. "Just like the pilgrims," we laughed.

Pat Benatar stuck around long enough to win our hearts and help whittle the turkey down to the carcass. As she and Neil left, I hoped the tryptophan wouldn't kick in and make her sleepy. In a few hours, Pat would be making her live concert debut in front of 3,000 people.

My worries evaporated as Pat Benatar hit the stage. She was a fireball of energy, tightly packed into a skin-tight spandex outfit. She strutted across the stage with attitude, making it clear that she'd arrived. Tonight, Pat was ready to prove herself. If I had any doubts whether this hot, young woman could rock the crowd, she immediately wiped them away. Pat took control of the stage from the moment she grabbed the mic and sang the first note. Her powerful voice soared over Neil Giraldo's guitar, singing anguished tales of hurtful, unfaithful lovers. Backed by a tight band, she delivered a hard rock punch that drove the audience into a frenzy.

Pat Benatar's debut album, *In The Heat of the Night*, became an instant hit and propelled her to the top echelons of rock stardom. Plus, she forged a path for the future, paving the way for female singers from Joan Jett to Melissa Etheridge and even Katy Perry. Benatar proved that women can be powerful and determined.

It's hard to believe that Pat Benatar has been eligible for induction into the Rock and Roll Hall of Fame since 2004. But, in one of the music industry's great injustices, she's been ignored. Despite the fact that Pat kicked the door open for strong, independent female singers, Benatar has not been voted into the hallowed hall. If Linda Ronstadt belongs in the Rock and Roll Hall of Fame, why not Pat Benatar?

Still, Benatar feels rewarded. In her memoir *Between A Rock And A Hard Place*, she is quoted as saying, "Every day since I was old enough to think, I've considered myself a feminist. It's empowering to watch and to know that, perhaps in some way, I made the hard path women have to walk just a little bit easier."

(l-r) KISW's Gary Crow, Mike West, Pat Benatar, Neil Giraldo, Beau Phillips

Chapter 31

PETE TOWNSHEND
GETS REVENGE

"No one knows what it's like to be the bad man,
to be the sad man…behind blue eyes."

The Who "Behind Blue Eyes"

It seems that every rock band endures feuds between its singer and lead guitarist, as if it's part of the script. Take Steven Tyler and Joe Perry. Both have been fired from or quit Aerosmith, and blamed each other. Eddie Van Halen dumped front man David Lee Roth, and then fired Sammy Hagar. Jon Bon Jovi canned guitarist Richie Sambora. Keith Richards has butted heads with Mick for decades. In fact, in his autobiography *Life,* Keith needled Jagger relentlessly and even implied that Mick was hung like a lawn jockey. The fighting Gallagher brothers famously bashed each other before breaking up their band, Oasis. Then there are the godfathers of hostile feuds, the Kinks' Ray and Dave Davies, who have bickered for years and broken up several times. Legend has it that Dave even spat on brother Ray during a concert.

But when it comes to love-hate relationships, Pete Townshend and Roger Daltrey are the undisputed champions. For more than fifty years, the Who's guitarist and singer have argued, taken breaks, recorded solo albums, reunited, then argued again. In the early stages of a band's career, it's healthy to have differing views. But over time, artists usually find common ground and set their egos aside.

Pete and Roger couldn't be more different. Townshend is tall, while Daltrey is vertically challenged. Pete's an intense workaholic who's deeply committed to new technology. Roger is more relaxed and doesn't even own a computer. Over the decades the singer and guitarist have played tug-of-war over everything from creative direction to concert set lists. Townshend wants to write and perform new songs, while Daltrey prefers singing the Who's greatest hits. But, whenever they are interviewed, Pete and Roger stick to the script and brush off their differences by saying they simply fight like all brothers do.

I got a taste of the tension between Roger Daltrey and Pete Townshend in 1982 while filming a TV interview with them in Chicago. I had an idea to film a TV interview special with Pete and Roger called WHO-TV that would air the evening before their upcoming concert. The band's record label made a formal request on my behalf. Meanwhile, I met with a TV station in Seattle in hopes of scoring a thirty-minute time slot—for free. A friend of mine worked at the station and arranged for me to meet with their general manager. As soon as I entered the GM's office, I knew I was in trouble. He stood up from behind his desk wearing a business suit and a cowboy hat. His office walls were plastered with pictures of him standing next to country music stars. Not a big Who fan. My friend introduced me, saying, "Beau is the manager of the number-one rock station in town." To which the GM snidely replied, "Son, being the number-one rock station is like being the world's tallest midget."

I let that comment pass, smiled and made my pitch: "Sir, I've read that you want to attract younger viewers. I have an idea that will help you attract thousands of 18 to 34 year olds."

Mister TV Cowboy sat back in his chair and responded, "Okay, I'm listening."

"The Who are a very popular rock band, and they're coming to Seattle in October for a sold-out concert for 40,000 fans." I went on to explain my plan to produce a special TV show called WHO-TV and air it on his station the night before the show. "Would you be interested in airing our WHO-TV special—at no cost to you?"

The general manager softened a bit and asked my friend for her opinion. She rushed to my defense. "The Who are a perfect fit for Channel 13. I think this is a great opportunity to attract a younger audience." The manager trusted my friend's opinion and reluctantly agreed to give me a free time slot from 10 to10:30 p.m. the evening before the Who concert. Victory!

Now all I had to do was convince the Who to let me interview the band, no simple feat. I put a call into Bill Curbishley, the Who's longtime manager. I left a message requesting permission to film brief interviews with Pete Townshend and Roger Daltrey. As I was babbling, Curbishley's assistant picked up the phone and said, "I heard your message, but Pete and Roger just aren't doing any interviews on this tour."

Undaunted, I countered, "I appreciate that their time is tight. But we're producing a WHO-TV special that can help them sell copies of their new album. Our Who program will air the night before their concert. Can I get just thirty minutes with Pete and Roger? I will make this very easy and can meet them in any city along the tour. We can film the interview at their hotel." Curbishley's assistant relented, sighing, "I doubt they'll do any interviews. But I'll ask Bill, and I'll get back to you."

I suspected she was just prolonging the agony and would call back with a "no." So I leaned on my friend at Warner Brothers, the Who's record label, for some added support. "I want to produce a TV show about the Who that will help you sell a ton of albums. It's a win-win for everyone. There's no cost to you, and I'll handle all of the details. Can you please call Bill Curbishley and help me book an interview with Pete and Roger?"

A few hand-wringing days passed. Then came the call came from the Who's management. Bill's assistant said, "Okay, you've got fifteen minutes with Pete and Roger on October 11th at 1 p.m. They will be staying at the Whitehall Hotel in Chicago. So you'll need to fly there and book a room at the Whitehall, and Pete and Roger will come to you for the interview."

I was shocked and thrilled. Before she could reconsider, I blurted out, "That's perfect, I'll get a room at the Whitehall and see them on October 11th." I wasn't sure how I'd turn fifteen minutes of interviews into a half-hour show. But I was so excited to score an exclusive interview with the Who, I'd figure out the details later. Time was running out, and I only had nine days to fly to Chicago, film the interviews, and create a TV program. No sweat.

I boarded a flight to Chicago and checked into my room at the Whitehall. I called around and found a local videographer who agreed to film the interview with Pete and Roger. I had thirty minutes to turn my hotel room into a TV set. With help from the cameraman, I pushed the bed and tables against the wall and positioned three armchairs facing each other. The video guy set up portable light panels and tripod-mounted video cameras. Meanwhile, I reviewed my questions on three-by-five cards and laid out a brand new Fender Stratocaster on my bed. It was red, just like the one Pete plays. I was hoping to get him to autograph it and offer the Strat as a contest prize inside the WHO-TV special. Guitarists can be picky about which guitars they autograph. Hopefully Townshend would be in a good mood.

The videographer and I were ready for the Who. Shortly after 1 p.m., there was a knock on my door. I rushed over and peeked through the eyehole. I saw a woman's face—and behind her stood Pete Townshend. I took a deep breath and opened the door. Jackie Curbishley extended her hand and introduced herself as Bill's wife. Today she was helping out by escorting Pete and Roger to the interview. Jackie stepped aside to let Pete pass and said, "Beau Phillips, meet Pete Townshend. Roger is on his way."

Townshend's face looked pale and gaunt. He seemed somber, didn't crack a smile and spoke softly. Pete looked weary. He had played a show the night before at the Rosemont Horizon, the first of the Who's two gigs in Chicago. I reached out to shake hands with Pete and noticed that his fingers looked red and battered, like ground beef. Pete is famous for smashing his guitars and violently slamming his hand against the guitar strings with powerful, windmill strokes. He gets so caught up in the music that his hands absorb tremendous punishment. And after decades of touring, his right hand looked battle-scarred. Pete would rather bleed than play with less passion.

Townshend settled into one armchair, and I sat across from him. He appeared sad and alone with his thoughts. A far cry from the man who'd be leaping around onstage that night before 20,000 fans.

Jackie reminded, "We only have fifteen minutes. Roger will be here soon. Maybe you should get started now with Pete."

"Okay, that's fine." I sat in the chair across from the great Pete Townshend, who was now looking a bit healthier under television lighting.

Now, Pete is wicked smart and has a reputation for being extremely sensitive. So, rather than ask him the typical interview questions ("tell me about your tour"), I went right to the most probing questions and asked, "Pete, I know that you and Keith Moon were very close. How have you dealt with his death?" He flinched and sat back in his chair, not expecting me to go there right away. But it must have triggered something in Townshend, and he immediately opened up. He leaned in closer, and I could see him thinking about how to answer. He spoke slowly and chose his words carefully. "Moonie was my brother. It's been three years, and I still haven't gotten over his death. We all knew he was self-destructive. But I was shocked. I still am."

Keith Moon literally drank himself to death. Ironically, he overdosed on Heminevrin (a drug used to curb alcohol abuse).

Knowing that Townshend was also a heavy drinker, I followed with, "Was Keith Moon's death a wake-up call for you?" Pete raised his head and stared at the ceiling for about ten seconds. Tears started to well up in his eyes. At that moment, there was a knock on my door. We turned off the cameras, and Jackie got up to welcome our next special guest.

She opened the door and in walked Roger Daltrey, one of rock's iconic voices. As he stood in the doorway, my knees trembled at the sight of Roger Daltrey and Pete Townshend together in *my* hotel room. I was among rock giants, two men who touched millions of fans and inspired hundreds of future rock singers, guitarists and air guitarists. This was going to be amazing! Pete and Roger *never* did interviews together. But today, I would capture them both on film. Or so I thought.

Daltrey took three steps into my room before noticing Townshend seated across the room. "What's this?" Roger asked. "I didn't know that he [Pete] would be here." And with that, he made a one-eighty, turned on his heels, and walked out

of the room. Jackie dashed after Roger, but he was not coming back. At least I had Townshend and Daltrey together for thirty seconds!

After Daltrey left, Pete snickered, "He can be such a pissant. But there's nobody else who I'd rather have sing my songs."

Jackie came back in the room out of breath and asked, "Pete, are you doing okay? Do you want to continue?" I froze. If Townshend ended the interview now, I was screwed. We hadn't recorded enough footage for a TV commercial, much less a half-hour show. So, I turned my eyes toward Pete, hoping that he'd continue. "No, I'm fine," Pete answered. "This is good." I sat back down across from him as the cameras rolled.

I picked up where we left off. Townshend talked more about losing Keith Moon. "I should have learned a lesson, but I didn't. I still drink too much." We were on a roll, and nobody seemed eager to stop. Jackie was on the phone, and I had plenty of questions left. So, Pete continued, "Many nights, if I couldn't find someone to sleep with, I'd sleep with my bottle of Rémy Martin." Then he confessed, "One night in London I drank so much that I almost died. My driver found me lying in the gutter, unconscious, and rushed me to the emergency room. Fortunately, the hospital staff heard that Pete Townshend was in the ER, and they ran to help me. One of the privileges of being famous, I guess. But if I was just an average bloke, I'd probably be dead."

It was painfully hard to watch one of your heroes so broken down by loss and booze. Pete was getting choked up. So, I lightened the mood and asked, "You've played songs like 'Baba O'Riley' and 'My Generation' hundreds of times. Do you ever get bored playing them?" Pete's answer was stunning. "Not at all. If I get tired of playing a song, I grab my guitar and find a quiet place. Then I play it over and over again

until I get back to the mental state I was in when I first wrote the song. I find that same fire again and it reconnects me."

Pete Townshend and I talked for forty-five minutes. He was entrancing and thoughtful, choosing his words carefully as any great writer would. I felt proud that I was able to keep Pete's interest and extract such candid comments. Of course, I wished I could have filmed Roger. But Pete was brilliant, and this footage would make a riveting television special. He stood up to leave, and I pushed my luck. "Pete, would you mind signing this Fender Strat? We'd like to give it away to a Who fan during this TV show." He smiled for the first time, grabbed the sharpie pen and wrote in bold letters, "Do not smash or burn this guitar. Love, Pete Townshend."

We shook hands and Pete left my room. I thanked him for his time and said it was too bad that Roger couldn't have joined us. Townshend grinned again and teased, "Come to the show tonight and watch what I do to him. I'll get my revenge." I closed the hotel room door and sat down with my videographer. He rewound the interview tape and we watched it from the beginning. We had captured powerful, gut-wrenching footage of Pete Townshend baring his soul. This would be an amazing TV special.

With the interview in the can, I drove to the concert, still re-playing Townshend's final comment in my head. What revenge would Pete take? I slapped the backstage pass on my jeans and entered the Rosemont Horizon before the doors opened to the public. The venue was empty except for a few roadies rolling equipment cases into place. The Rosemont felt more like an airplane hangar than a concert hall. In fact, it may have been a hangar at one time since the Rosemont was across the street from Chicago's O'Hare Airport.

The Who was onstage, rehearsing a new song called "Eminence Front" from their latest album, *It's Hard*. Townshend

sang lead vocals on the tune, so Roger took a break and was sitting on a drum riser. During the sound check, the band seemed very relaxed. After playing together for decades, the Who didn't need to rehearse much. This was just to get the right sound mix for the barn-like hall. As Townshend sang the refrain, he changed the words from "eminence front" to "ignorant cunt." The sadness was gone and Pete was onstage in his comfort zone. Too bad I didn't get that on film.

The band retreated to their backstage dressing rooms as the doors were unlocked and the crowd packed into the Rosemont Horizon. For the first few songs, I was allowed to watch from the photo pit, right in front of the stage. It's that narrow gap with a barricade that separates the stage and the crowd. Townshend, dressed in a black leather jacket, looked much tougher than he did in my hotel room. I was less than fifteen feet from Pete Townshend, standing right below him. The crowd was going insane behind me as Townshend opened the show with a familiar guitar lick. But it wasn't from "Substitute," the song they routinely started with. Roger didn't notice at first that Pete was actually playing "I Can't Explain" instead. So Daltrey stepped up to the mic and started to sing the opening line of "Substitute" before he finally noticed that Pete had tripped him up. Roger looked over at Townshend and mouthed the words,

During their 1982 American tour, the Who's opening song was an early hit called "Substitute," followed by "I Can't Explain." They played these two songs, in the same order, every night... except for this show in Chicago. After doing 40-plus shows together, using the same set list, Pete decided to mix it up—and throw off Roger in the process.

"What the fuck?" Pete smiled as if to say, "This is payback for walking out this afternoon." Daltrey shot him a nasty look, grabbed the mic again…and flubbed the first line of the song. Townshend laughed at Roger and winked at me, knowing that he'd gotten revenge for Daltrey's hissy fit.

Townshend wrote (and Daltrey sang) "I hope I die before I get old" in their classic "My Generation." Pete recently clarified his famous line in *Rolling Stone*, saying, "I hope I die while I still feel this alive, this young, this healthy, this happy, and this fulfilled. But I may get creaky, cranky, get cancer, and die in some hospice with a massive resentment against everyone I leave behind. But I am not old yet. If getting older means I continue to cherish the lessons every passing day brings, more and more, then whatever happens, I think I'll be happy to die before I get old, or after I get old, or anytime in between. I sound like a fucking greeting card!"

In 2014, both Pete Townshend and Roger Daltrey turned seventy. To no one's surprise, the Who spit in the face of aging and plan to celebrate their 50th anniversary by performing a world tour.

Chapter 32

JAGGER AND
THE JACKASS

"Anything worth doing is worth overdoing."

Mick Jagger

I transitioned out of radio in the mid-90s to try my hand at cable television. I was recruited by my friend Andy Schuon, who was then MTV's executive VP of Programming. Andy confided, "We're going to blow up VH1 and start over. We'd like you to move to New York and be the head of marketing and promotion for the 'new' VH1." It was hard to say no to joining MTV Networks. And I was ready for a bigger challenge. So, I moved to the Connecticut suburbs and steeled myself for the 116-mile roundtrip commute into Times Square.

On my first day at VH1, I showed up for work promptly at 8 a.m....and was the only person on the 20th floor. I walked through darkened hallways, past empty cubicles, until I found my new home, a corner office overlooking Times Square. A few people straggled in around 9 a.m., and the floor was buzzing with activity by 10 a.m. Lesson number one: people start late and work late.

Moments later, VH1's president, John Sykes, came in to welcome me and said, "Sorry for the short notice, but we have a meeting in an hour with Michael Cohl, the Rolling Stones' tour promoter. Think of some ideas that we can pitch to him."

Cohl had a reputation as a shrewd negotiator. He is often credited with reinventing the concert business, raking in huge sums from tour sponsors and inflating concert ticket prices to new heights. It's been reported that Cohl got the job as the Stones' promoter by pitching Mick Jagger. The story goes that Mick once asked Michael, "If you become our tour promoter, you stand to get very rich. Why should we hire you?" To which Cohl replied, "Because I know God." Jagger smiled, and the deal was done.

"Sure, John. No problem."

"This is a cool first assignment," I thought, pulling out a fresh notepad. I started scribbling down ways that VH1 could attach itself to the Stones. The band had just released their *Voodoo Lounge* album, so I wrote that down. I looked at the band's tour schedule and circled some key dates. Then I noted a few promotional ideas that would get fans excited, gain attention for VH1, and help Michael Cohl sell concert tickets. After all, that's why he was seeing us.

Sykes and I showed up at the Four Seasons Hotel at 11 a.m. for our meeting with Michael Cohl. We sat in the meeting room that was adjacent to Cohl's penthouse suite. Then we waited.

When Michael finally entered the room, he looked like he'd just rolled out of bed. In a white bathrobe wrapped over an undershirt, he needed a shave and shower. We sat across the conference table from Cohl, feeling overdressed in sport coats and slacks.

Cohl looked straight at us and opened with, "Let's do this. The Stones are touring this year. What can you do to help me sell tickets?"

"First," Sykes began, "we'd like to host a live, pay-per-view simulcast in conjunction with our Showtime. We project 750,000 subscribers at $19.95 each." Cohl showed the hint of a smile. "Then, we'll repackage the concert for a VH1 special."

"Good," he noted. "What else?"

I stepped in, "We also want to do a national promotion."

"Whaddaya got?" Cohl barked as he scratched his stubbly cheek.

"Michael, I've got a few ideas. As you know, the Stones' VooDoo Lounge Tour will hit forty cities in the U.S. We'd like to do a national contest and select one winner in each city. We will partner with rock radio stations in each city to choose one person who would go out on stage and introduce the Rolling Stones. That person would get to make the six-word announcement that every fan wants to say: 'Ladies and Gentlemen, the Rolling Stones!' What do you think?"

"No."

"No?" I asked, feeling deflated. "Can we discuss it?"

"No. What's your next idea?" Cohl snapped.

I regrouped and started again. "We hear that the Stones will perform the song "Honky Tonk Women" on tour. Of course, that song features a cowbell. So, we'd like to put a guest cowbell player onstage with the Stones each night to…"

"No," Cohl interrupted. "Next idea?"

"Okay." I collected my thoughts. Last chance. "The Stones are playing at Joe Robbie Stadium in Miami on November 25th. That's the day after Thanksgiving. So, we'd like to offer fans a bucket list experience. We'll search for the big-

gest Stones fan and fly the winner to Miami for a Thanksgiving feast—a "Beggars Banquet"—with the Stones."

I hadn't heard a "no" yet from Cohl, so I kept going. "We'd set up a dinner table on the fifty-yard line and..."

"I like it!" Cohl jumped in again. "In fact, I'll go you one better. Your winner can fly from Tampa to Miami with the Stones, on their private jet."

"No shit?" I gasped. "That would be amazing."

"Write it up and send your proposal to my office," he ordered. Sykes and I quickly stood up and shook hands with Michael. Then we left before he could change his mind.

The VH1 promotion team started assembling the details of our Beggars Banquet promotion, borrowing the title from the Stones' 1968 album. We ran a nationwide promotion, searching for America's biggest Rolling Stones fan. We teased viewers with the chance to fly to Miami with the Rolling Stones on their private jet, then share a Thanksgiving feast with Mick, Keith, Ronnie and Charlie on the fifty-yard line of the Dolphins' football stadium. That evening, the contest winner would watch the concert from great seats and get backstage passes to the VooDoo Lounge. It was a Stones fan's wildest fantasy, assuming the winner was a Stones fan. Too bad that our winner wasn't.

Thousands of entries poured in as fans detailed why they deserved to win this trip of a lifetime. About 99 percent of the entries came in the form of a letter. But one guy from Iowa submitted a beautiful line drawing of the Rolling Stones. Richard Wongo showed a lot of skill in the way he captured the band's likeness with an ink pen. Our team conferred and agreed that the artist from Iowa showed the most creativity, and he was awarded the Thanksgiving feast with the Rolling Stones.

I flew to Tampa to escort our winner and met him inside the airport. Standing near the gate, I watched as people exited the flight from Topeka. I played a little game with myself, guessing which guy might be our Stones winner. A few minutes passed, then a dopey-looking character came through the jetway wearing a fringed, buckskin jacket. He was tall and thin, with curly brown hair held down by a Rolling Stones cap. That's my guy!

I walked up and introduced myself. He stuck out a sweaty hand: "I'm Richard Wongo." We strolled to the far end of the terminal and found the gate that led to the Stones' private plane. As we boarded, I explained my plan to our win-

For years, MTV offered "flyaway" trips such as this one. Viewers were tempted by enticing promos à la "You and a friend will fly on a private jet to see Madonna in Las Vegas." What contestants didn't realize was that the value of such a trip must be claimed as income. It's taxable. We'd explain to the winners, "You've won roundtrip airfare to Vegas on a private jet, one hotel room and a rental car. That's a total value of $40,000."

"Wow!", winners would exclaim.

"However", we'd add. "You're responsible for paying about $12,000 in taxes to the IRS."

This was usually met with, "What? I can't afford $12,000."

"Well, here's another option" (a line that never failed). "It costs a lot to charter a private jet for forty-eight hours. Instead, you can fly first class to Las Vegas and save $11,000 in taxes." I don't think any winner ever chose the private jet.

229

ner. "We have a short flight to Miami. So, once we reach altitude, I'll bring you over to meet Mick Jagger. You might have some questions ready."

There were probably forty people on board the full-sized jet, including the band and their entourage. The seats were all wider and further apart than on a typical 747. I sat with Wongo in the middle of the plane, about ten rows behind Jagger. I learned that Richard was thirty-two, worked in construction and lived in Davenport. "Are you excited?" I asked.

"Kinda," said Mr. Wongo, not much of a conversationalist.

After the plane leveled off, I leaned over and told our winner, "It's time." We stood up and headed toward the row where Mick was seated. Jagger looked aristocratic and rail thin, dressed in a navy sport coat and black jeans. As the Rolling Stones' designated business driver, he was sifting through a stack of file folders when Wongo and I approached. "Hi Mick, I'm Beau Phillips from VH1. Do you have a few minutes to meet 'America's biggest Stones fan'?"

"Sure," he answered as he removed his reading glasses. "Have a seat." Wongo took the empty seat next to Mick while I stood in the aisle. I found it interesting that Mick did all of the talking. Our winner was either tongue-tied or had nothing to say. Then, Jagger asked, "So you are America's biggest Rolling Stones fan. What's your favorite song?"

Our winner thought for a moment, then stammered, "Uhhh. I can't really think of one. I guess I'm not much of a Rolling Stones fan."

Wongo sat there staring blankly at the world's most famous rock singer—as my blood boiled. I imagined the tongue-lashing that I'd get from Michael Cohl. And I wouldn't blame him. I was standing next to Mick Jagger in the aisle, ready to clobber Richard Wongo with a tray table. Jagger glared at

me as I grabbed our idiot winner by the shirt, yanking him into the aisle and dragging him back to our seats. Exasperated, I asked him, "You couldn't think of one Rolling Stones song? My mom can name a Stones song! Ever heard of 'Satisfaction'? You're supposed to be the biggest Stones fan! You got to meet the most famous rock singer in the world. And you tell him that you're not really a fan? Are you insane?"

"Sorry," Wongo mumbled.

Incredulous, I didn't let up. "What about the beautiful Stones picture that you drew?"

"I like to draw," Richard replied.

"What about your Stones cap?"

"My friend loaned it to me."

Totally bewildered, I asked, "Why did you enter the contest if you're not a fan?"

Wongo shrugged and hung his head. "I dunno."

We landed in Miami and I drove Mr. Wongo to Joe Robbie Stadium, where VH1's staff took over. As promised, Richard did share a Thanksgiving table with the Stones, but he sat at the opposite end from the band, by himself. Understandably, the band wanted nothing to do with him.

That evening at the concert, Jagger whipped the stadium crowd to a frenzy. The Stones played hit after hit for two hours and then brought guest singers on stage including Sheryl Crow and Bo Diddley. Lucky me, I sat next to Richard Wongo, who seemed thoroughly bored. After the final encore, I handed him an envelope that contained his backstage credentials, fulfilling my obligation to this faux fan. I explained, "These are passes to the Stones' VooDoo Lounge. It's a private backstage after-party, with free food

and booze. I heard that Ronnie Wood and Keith Richards are supposed to stop by. So, I'll see you inside."

The concert ended and I made my way back to the VooDoo Lounge. Wongo never showed up. It was just as well.

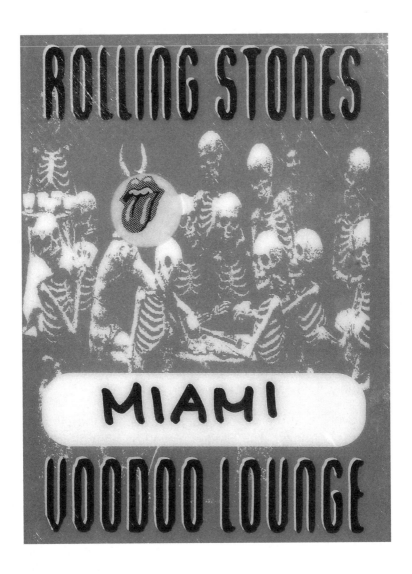

Chapter 33

THE LIFE AND DEATH
OF IRONHORSE

"When you get successful, you can do pretty much
whatever you want."

Randy Bachman

You've never heard of the band Ironhorse. That's understandable, because the band's career in the U.S. lasted exactly one hour. I witnessed their anticipated debut (and subsequent demise) at the Grand Hyatt Hotel in Atlanta.

Legend has it that Led Zeppelin got its name when the Who's Keith Moon told Jimmy Page that his new band would go over like a "lead balloon." On this night, Canada's Ironhorse

I've mentioned before how the choice of songs that got played on rock radio stations was heavily influenced by a small group of radio program directors. About twenty in all, we all worked with Lee Abrams, a respected rock consultant. Collectively, Lee and the PDs chose the songs that were on the most popular rock stations in America.

went down like, well, an iron horse. Former Guess Who and Bachman Turner Overdrive front man Randy Bachman formed the band in Vancouver, Canada. After BTO broke up, Randy assembled Ironhorse and wrote most of their songs.

Lee Abrams's annual meeting for program directors, known as the Superstars Radio Conference, attracted the nation's top rock programmers. Our days at the meeting were spent sequestered in conference rooms, dissecting the latest trends. After dinner, many of us would split off in search of fun.

Ironhorse's record label, Atlantic Records, hoped to arrange a showcase performance for the radio elite while they were all in one hotel. The label knew that if these radio execs were impressed, it would light a fire that might spread nationwide. So, Atlantic contacted Abrams and pitched, "What would it take to have Ironhorse perform privately for your PDs?"

Lee pondered that question as the label exec sweetened the deal, eager to close. "How about if I throw in an ounce of blow?" Bingo. A deal was made. The radio PDs, me included, would attend an Ironhorse performance, and a large bag of cocaine was delivered in the dead of night. Allegedly. Our fearless leader approached me and my radio band of brothers with an enticing offer. "I'd like you to come to the Ironhorse performance tonight. And to make it worth your while, they've given us some party powder to get everyone in the right mood." It wasn't a hard sell. But after being cooped up in meeting rooms all day, seeing Ironhorse wasn't high on my list.

An hour before showtime, I wasn't shy about borrowing the powder-filled baggie and disappearing into the men's room...several times. By 8 p.m., I dutifully settled in with the other radio guys to watch the debut of Ironhorse. Needless to say, I was "up" for the show.

Atlantic Records staged a private concert, but it wasn't exactly intimate. A small stage was constructed in the cavernous hotel ballroom that was designed to accommodate 1,000 people. The radio guys and I sat in folding chairs, clustered together in the center of the ballroom. The seats

were lined up in a straight line, side by side, facing the stage. Seated twenty across, we felt less like fans, and more like jurors. Tonight, we would pass judgment on an artist's career. With no fans to cheer on the band, the room was dead quiet. Surrounded by emptiness in the sterile ballroom, we sat in silence and waited for Ironhorse.

The chandeliers dimmed and the spotlight hit Randy Bachman as Ironhorse shuffled on stage. We all respected Bachman's work with BTO and applauded. He'd written huge hits. But Randy looked burnt out. Never a small man, he had packed on some pounds. I was close enough to see that Randy was already sweating.

I was mildly curious to hear his new band. Unfortunately, that curiosity evaporated quickly. A few songs into the set, we couldn't help but notice that Ironhorse songs sounded a lot like BTO's. Not surprising when you consider that Bachman was Ironhorse's songwriter, guitarist and founder. But these regurgitated songs sounded like bad BTO covers. I whispered to the guy next to me, "Doesn't this song sound just like 'Takin' Care of Business?' " He answered, "Yeah, and the last one had the same guitar riff as 'You Ain't Seen Nothing Yet.' " This led to more snarky comments, such as, "Remember Randy's old band, Bachman-Turner Overweight?"

As each song ended, we sat on our hands and didn't applaud. Okay, a few people gave courtesy claps. But there weren't enough to sound convincing. The silence was deafening, not to mention embarrassing, as the sparse applause echoed throughout the oversized ballroom. We were seated about fifty feet from the stage. Close enough for Randy Bachmann to read our faces. And nobody looked happy. Granted, radio programmers can be a tough crowd to please. But this was as bad as it gets, even with the nose candy.

I sat there patiently while Ironhorse stumbled down the stretch. Thirty minutes into the set, a few radio guys slipped out of the ballroom between songs. I suppose they honored their agreement to give Bachman a fair listen. I would have felt uncomfortable just walking out. So, I decided to endure Ironhorse until they crossed the finish line. Mercifully, the show ended a few songs later. About half of us remained, feeling somewhat obliged after draining the cocaine supply.

Randy Bachman is a tremendous songwriter and guitarist who was used to hearing thunderous ovations. But on this night, he didn't take care of business, and Ironhorse's career in America went off the rails. One and done.

Chapter 34

FREEBIRD FLIES
IN CLEVELAND

"Take your time. Don't live too fast.
Troubles will come and they will pass."

Lynyrd Skynyrd "Simple Man"

On the night of Lynyrd Skynyrd's tragic plane crash, I was a twenty-five-year old rock radio DJ on KYA-FM in San Francisco. It was the evening of October 20, 1977, and I was just settling in for my five-hour show when the studio hotline rang. It was a radio friend of mine who worked in Atlanta. He sounded frantic and asked, "Have you heard about Lynyrd Skynyrd?"

"No. What about them?" I asked, while cueing up the next record.

"Their plane crashed somewhere in Mississippi," he said breathlessly. The band was on their way to a concert, but their plane crashed in the woods."

"Holy shit!" I swung my feet off the console and sprang into action. "Will you go on the air with me and talk to my audience?" I asked the Atlanta jock.

"Sure," he offered.

I had never been in the position of covering breaking news like this and went with my first instinct. After the song end-

ed, I broke in and put my friend on the air, live. He identified himself as a DJ on WKLS, 6 Rock in Atlanta and drawled, "Lynyrd Skynyrd had just finished their concert in Greenville, South Carolina, a few hours northeast of Atlanta. From what we're being told, the band members were flying in a small plane headed for their next gig in Baton Rouge, Louisiana. But the plane flew too low and crashed in the forest near McComb, Mississippi."

I asked the obvious question: "Was anybody hurt?"

"It's still dark at the crash site," he said. "We hear there were some serious injuries. But we're told that everyone survived."

I talked about Lynryd Skynyrd's plane crash throughout the evening. As a fan of Skynyrd's music myself, I empathized with callers about how fortunate they were to survive a plane crash. I put listeners on the air who knew the band or had stories to share. At the time, we had no wire service, no TV in the studio, and Al Gore's internet was years away. I was on my own and went with what I had, which wasn't much. I foolishly relied on the secondhand account of another DJ.

Sadly, the plane crash came at the peak of the band's career. Ironically, Lynyrd Skynyrd had released their album *Street Survivors* just three days earlier. It was their best album yet, and the cover featured a haunting photograph of the band members engulfed in flames. One new song, "That Smell," was particularly disturbing. Singer Ronnie Van Zant wailed *"the smell of death surrounds you."* How ironic that Van Zant and several of his bandmates would die in a flaming crash only days after the album's release. MCA Records quickly noticed that morbid coincidence, and the original album cover was soon pulled from store shelves and replaced with a different image.

It wasn't until the next morning that I realized how wrong my jock buddy had been. I passed a newsstand and saw the *San Francisco Chronicle* headline, "Members of Rock Band Killed in Plane Crash." I felt stunned... and stupid. In my haste to break the Skynyrd story to San Franciscans, I blew it. I was still pretty green, and my friend claimed to have accurate info. But no excuses. I should have double-checked my sources before opening my mouth. The memory of Lynyrd Skynyrd's plane crash disturbed me for many years. Not only was I devastated by the tragedy, I could never shake my failure under pressure. I learned a hard lesson that night.

Skynyrd's plane ran out of fuel less than an hour from their final destination and crashed while attempting to make an emergency landing. Singer Ronnie Van Zant and guitarist Steve Gaines were killed, along with their backup singer, road manager and both pilots. The surviving band members all suffered serious injuries. They healed physically, but were emotionally scarred for life.

In the summer of 1996, my friend Josh Simons invited me to Cleveland for the premiere of *Freebird, the Movie.* It's a Lynyrd Skynyrd concert film, shot at two of the band's final appearances—the Knebworth festival in England and the Oakland Coliseum in California. *Freebird* captured singer Ronnie Van Zant at his southern-fried best. Make no mistake, he was the band's spiritual leader. Losing Ronnie in the plane crash was a punch to the gut that took the air out of Lynyrd Skynyrd, and the band never fully recovered.

The highlight of *Freebird, the Movie* is the final eleven minutes. The film's producers had gotten hold of the handheld

Super 8 camera, recovered from the crash site that the band had used to film their antics onboard the plane. These private home movies caught Skynyrd's playful side as they mugged for the camera. This shaky, extremely rare footage had never been seen before. Almost 20 years after the crash, their fans would watch those chilling final moments at the end of *Freebird, the Movie.*

The Super 8 film had not been touched in more than eighteen years. That's a bad thing. Over time, film layers begin to separate and degrade. The producers learned that the best way to preserve the film required a delicate baking technique. The film was literally baked inside an oven for several hours at a very low temperature. This heating process temporarily bonded the film layers together long enough to allow creation of a digital master copy. This was a risky move. But it was the only hope to save Lynyrd Skynyrd's airplane footage.

Freebird, the Movie was screened for a who's-who crowd of TV, radio and newspaper reporters at a private theater inside the Rock and Roll Hall of Fame in Cleveland. I was invited to the event and decided this might be my chance to get closure nearly two decades after Skynyrd's fateful night.

Eighteen years after that fateful plane crash, I was alarmed by how frail the surviving band members looked. Their eyes seemed sunken and hollow. You could tell that they'd cheated death and left a part of their soul in the Mississippi woods. Guitarist Gary Rossington had a vacant stare and seemed like a shell of the man who once powered Lynyrd Skynyrd's three-guitar attack. Bassist Leon Wilkeson walked tentatively with the help of a cane and sat down slowly at the front table. Keyboardist Billy Powell's face was pale and drawn, as if he was still in shock. The healthiest looking member was drummer Artimus Pyle.

Also on hand was Leonard Skinner, the band's namesake and Ronnie's former high school gym teacher in Jacksonville, Florida. Leonard told me, "Those boys gave me nothing but trouble, and I hated their long hair. So I kept sending Ronnie to the principal's office."

In retaliation for Leonard Skinner's hard-line discipline, Van Zant named his band after Skinner, just to spite him. The spelling was changed to avoid legal issues.

The four surviving band members had agreed to appear at a press conference prior to the showing. They fielded questions from TV, radio and newspaper reporters, speaking in hushed tones. The remaining members sat alongside Ronnie Van Zant's widow, Judy, and Johnny Van Zant, who stepped in to fill his big brother's shoes. As usual, the journalists picked old scabs and asked the Skynyrd boys about the plane crash. The band dutifully answered the same questions they'd heard a million times over the past 18 years. Their responses were mumbled and delivered with no emotion.

Then, one reporter asked the guys, "Have you seen this film yet?"

The four men looked at each other, lowered their eyes and shook their heads. None of them had. And it was obvious that they were uncomfortable about reliving the nightmare of October 20, 1977.

After the press conference, the doors opened to a small theater inside the Rock and Roll Hall of Fame. The guests, a combination of VIPs, film producers, media reporters and band members, quietly filed in and took their seats. For those in attendance, the mood was somber and uncomfortable as we ignored the elephant in the room. Everyone

in the theater knew this was the first time that Lynyrd Skynyrd's surviving members would see footage of the band's final moments together.

Interestingly, the remaining band members did not sit together to watch the movie. Maybe it was still too painful. Gary, Billy, Leon and Artimus were seated in different parts of the theater, and other guests left them alone with their thoughts. The theater lights dimmed and the film's title filled the screen. The opening credits were accompanied by home movies of the guys goofing around backstage. Artimus Pyle had filmed himself walking onto the plane, into the cockpit, and to his seat. No doubt it was shot on the same handheld camera that was recovered from the wreckage. There was a moving clip of singer Ronnie Van Zant on the plane, alternately playing poker and staring out of the window. He'd gaze outside, looking deep in thought. Then Ronnie would lean over to place his bet, then return to pensively looking out the window. You couldn't help but wonder what was on his mind.

Then, the film shifted gears and swept down on the Knebworth Festival in England as Lynyrd Skynyrd took the stage. The concert opened with a bang as the band tore into "Workin' For MCA," followed by their first hit, "I Ain't The One." Lynyrd Skynyrd was in total command as Ronnie Van Zant prowled back and forth, singing barefoot so he could feel the heat of the stage. The band sizzled onstage and was clearly having fun, in stark contrast to the subdued tone inside the Rock and Roll Hall of Fame. Looking around in the darkened theater, I could see the band members watching intently. On the big screen, Skynyrd kicked it up a notch with "Gimme Three Steps" and their classic, "Sweet Home Alabama." Fittingly, the concert ended with a scorching twelve-minute three-guitar jam of the band's signature song, "Freebird."

After ninety minutes of brilliant performance footage, *Freebird, the Movie* delivered its money shot, saved for last. Inside the theater, the crowd leaned forward, and I could feel the tension mount. We dreaded what was about to happen. While Skynyrd's onboard movie camera did not film the actual crash, it did capture the band's final moments together before their plane went down. Together we watched as the guys took turns filming one another and making faces at the camera. There was no hint of tension, just scenes of a rock band letting off steam after a show. Fade to black.

As the lights came up, I looked around the theater. There was an unmistakable heaviness in the theater, and nobody spoke a word. Ronnie Van Zant's widow, Judy, who produced the movie, was visibly moved. While she'd seen the chilling footage many times, watching it alongside Ronnie's bandmates struck a raw nerve. Seated a few rows away, I saw Gary Rossington being consoled by his wife, Dale Krantz, a background singer who was also in the crash. Billy Powell and Leon Wilkeson had tears in their eyes and walked out silently, and alone.

The last person to leave was Artimus Pyle. He escaped the plane crash with the fewest injuries. In fact, Pyle was credited for leaving the crash site and running to get help for his friends. Reliving that moment must have been more than he could take. With his head buried in his hands, Artimus sat in his seat and cried uncontrollably, shaking his head from side to side. Everyone around him was respectful and allowed Skynyrd's drummer to grieve alone. I felt a lump in my throat watching Pyle's emotional release.

The surviving members of Lynyrd Skynyrd still tour frequently, with Ronnie's kid brother Johnny Van Zant on vocals. Leon Wilkeson, Billy Powell and Artimus Pyle died several years after the *Freebird* premiere. Gary Rossington still performs and carries on as the last original member of Lynyrd Skynyrd.

For years, Skynyrd honored their fallen bandmates in concert by performing an instrumental version of the song "Freebird." The band played the music without a lead singer. The musicians stood in the shadows while a lone spotlight shone down on the microphone at center stage, in a silent tribute to Ronnie Van Zant. *"If I leave here tomorrow, would you still remember me?"*

Chapter 35

DEF LEPPARD
HITS THE BEACH

"I feel the need, the need for speed."

Tom Cruise "Top Gun"

The year was 1983, the year of Def Leppard. If it weren't for Michael Jackson's *Thriller*, their album *Pyromania* would have been the top seller that year. The five blokes from Sheffield, England, took the rock world by storm with whale-catching hooks and rugged guitars. During that summer, Def Leppard swarmed every car radio, blasting stadium-rock anthems like "Photograph," "Rock of Ages" and "Foolin'".

By the time Def Leppard organized a U.S. concert tour, it was already being hailed as the "new British Invasion." Ironically, the band's tour dates had been booked long before *Pyromania* was released. And back then, Def Leppard was just another warm-up band looking for a break. So they were happy to join Billy Squier's tour as the opening act. In the months that followed, Def Leppard's career kicked into overdrive, and their popularity was exploding. In fact, they had grown even hotter than Billy Squier, which caused many to question who the real headliner was.

Billy Squier was riding high until he released a song called "Rock Me Tonite". It was a pretty good tune, but the companion video killed Billy's credibility. Apparently Squier never got the memo that unless they could shake it like Steven Ty-

ler, rock stars shouldn't dance. Unfortunately, Billy showed his stuff in the "Rock Me Tonite" video and demonstrated to the world that he moved more like Mickey Mouse than Mick Jagger. Dressed in a pink tank top, Squier rolled around on a bed, which fueled rumors that he was gay. Even if those rumors were untrue, the scene gave a whole new meaning to his famous lyric, "Stroke me, stroke me."

It may be lonely at the top. But it's a bitch at the bottom. When the Billy Squier / Def Leppard tour hit Seattle, the bands' fortunes had reversed 180 degrees. What started as a spark of embarrassment for Billy Squier burst into a full-blown dumpster fire that incinerated his career. Meanwhile, Def Leppard's moment had arrived, and it was the hottest band in America.

By sheer coincidence, Def Lep's concert date was scheduled during Seattle's Seafair celebration. Seafair is a city-wide summer festival that culminates with hydroplane races. More than 500,000 people line the shores of Lake Washington to watch the powerboats and if they're lucky, bathe in some rare sunshine.

In 1983, KISW decided to get into the Seafair spirit, and we wanted to go big. So, we jumped in with both feet. We were a band of renegades who tended to zig while everyone else zagged. So, rather than just talking about the races like other stations, KISW decided to enter our own hydroplane in the big race. We didn't care if our boat was competitive. This was all about having fun with our listeners!

With the bar set extremely low, we asked around about buying a used hydroplane. We quickly learned that it's almost impossible to find one. But after some serious digging, we found a grizzled hydroplane veteran named Fred Leyland who gave us hope. "Yeah, I've got an old hydroplane that's been collecting dust for years. Hell, I don't even know if it

runs anymore. But you're welcome to it. I'll let you have it for 500 bucks. But you've got to haul it out of here."

Considering that professional hydroplane teams invested millions in their boats, $500 seemed like a fair deal. Clearly, if we wanted to enter a boat in the Seafair race, this relic was our only option. As we dragged it out into the sunlight, the news got worse. This hunk of junk needed a lot of work. The owner added, "When she did run, that damn boat was the loudest, slowest, heaviest boat in the field."

"Perfect. We'll take it." Three of us hitched the rusted boat and trailer to our van and drove the old girl back to the radio station. Now we needed to clean off years of neglect and find a sucker willing to drive our hydroplane on Seafair Sunday.

We recruited some mechanics to work on the hunk of junk's engine while the station staff spent evenings sanding her hull. As it turned out, the engine did still run…but barely. A local shop slapped on a fresh coat of black paint and our boat looked almost presentable. Now it was time to lower the hydroplane into the water and see what she could do. During its test runs, our boat was so heavy that it sat low in the water and slogged along. While newer hydroplanes, equipped with turbine engines, skimmed along the water, our motor sounded like a fork that got stuck in a garbage disposal. You could hear our big, black boat chugging from miles away.

We shined her up like a new dime and named our hydroplane the "Miss Rock." On-air, our jocks announced that KISW's big, black beast would be racing on Seafair Sunday. We joked that Miss Rock was powered by gerbils and had "eight speeds of slow." While the other entries were well-oiled corporate machines, ours was the true party boat of Seafair. Of course, it had no prayer of winning. But that

wasn't the point. We wanted to be the underdog that everyone would root for. And boy did they.

In the days leading up to the big race, KISW displayed our vessel at high-traffic spots all over town. We invited Seattleites to become part of our extended racing team and sign her hull. People flocked to see our hydroplane and apply their autographs. By the time Miss Rock hit the water on Seafair Sunday, she proudly bore more than 10,000 signatures. But we saved room for five more.

KISW had been early supporters of Def Leppard, and we got to know the band before they were all the rage. In fact, Joe Elliott often sent handwritten notes to us on hotel stationery from the road. Just to say hi.

The city was abuzz over Def Leppard's sold-out concert scheduled for that same week, right after the hydroplane races. We called Joe Elliott and his bandmates at their hotel and welcomed them to town. As it happened, they had a day off and had decided to hang around Seattle for the entire weekend. We invited the band to join us for some sun at the beach. "Why don't you guys come down to the pit area tomorrow and add your signatures to our hydroplane? Then you can christen Miss Rock!"

The band loved the idea and agreed to meet in the pit area at noon. On-air, we enthusiastically promoted Def Leppard's appearance and invited fans to come down and watch the band christen Miss Rock.

Twenty-four hours before the big race, the fab five arrived at the beach. The crowd cheered as they signed their names to the bottom of Miss Rock's hull. When it came time to christen the hydroplane, Def Leppard used prop bottles, like

the fake bottles used in movie bar fights. If we'd used a real bottle of champagne, the thick glass would have probably smashed through the hull. So, we wisely bought thin, breakable bottles that were made of sugar, like candy shells. At the christening, I filled Joe Elliott's fake bottle with water, and it started melting immediately. The sugar bottle was literally disintegrating. Sweating bullets, I remembered that we'd brought a spare. So I quickly filled the second prop bottle, handed it to Joe and ordered, "Swing it now!" Def Leppard's singer grabbed the bottle by its neck and triumphantly smacked it across the hydroplane's bow. Then he added a special twist. "I hereby christen this boat the "Miss Rock of Ages." The crowd went wild.

With our hydroplane officially christened, the band members looked at me as if to say, "Now, how do we get out of here?" Somehow, I hadn't expected 2,000 fans to show up. The hydroplane pit area was only designed to accommodate 100 people. I should have realized that Def Leppard were hugely popular chick magnets and hired security guys. Once the band got into the pit area, they were surrounded by a screaming mob, with no escape route. Ooops.

Before the fans could mobilize, I opened the rear door of KISW's van and the band members piled in. I instructed our summer intern, "Be careful, you're driving the biggest band in the world." Slowly, the crowd parted, and the van forged ahead. Once Def Leppard had safely cleared the pit area, Miss Rock headed for her appearance at the Seafair Torchlight Parade. On this night, she'd join eight other eight hydroplanes rolling through the streets of downtown Seattle.

On Seafair Sunday morning, Miss Rock was ready to rock the racecourse. Throngs of fans packed the beach, and hundreds of boats lined the log boom that surrounded the course. The Miss Rock was little more than a motorized buoy, and we knew that. It was part of her appeal.

After weeks of preparation, Miss Rock approached the starting line along with four turbo-charged hydroplanes. The starting gun sounded, and in no time Miss Rock took her spot in last place. The professional hydroplanes skipped over the waves at 200 mph while our tugboat churned through the water like an egg beater, doing a solid 85. Fans went crazy and raised their beers every time she chugged by. Ironically, the TV cameras focused more on our slow-moving fan favorite than on the Miller- and Budweiser-sponsored "beer boats." In our minds, that was victory enough.

Sadly, getting christened by Def Leppard was Miss Rock's finest moment. The boat's motor sputtered, coughed and finally died in the first race—then burst into flames. Literally, smoke on the water. Miss Rock bobbed aimlessly in the middle of the course and started to list. Rescue boats zoomed to her aid, put out the fire and attached a towrope before she could sink. As our flaming hull limped back to the pit area, our driver climbed out of the cockpit and stood on the blackened hull, with his arms raised triumphantly. That brought more roars from the crowd. Our parched driver sat down and accepted beers from the fans who swam out to greet him. He popped off the cap of one and toasted onlookers, which brought more hooting and hollering from the beach.

That night, Def Leppard (and Billy Squier) capped the day with an amazing show. And Miss Rock was retired to a local scrap yard. Maybe next year.

Def Leppard stands in front of KISW's Miss Rock hydroplane.
(l-r) Joe Elliott holding the prop bottle he used to christen Miss Rock,
Phil Collen, KISW's Steve Slaton, Rick Allen, fan, Rick Savage
and Steve Clark)

Epilogue

While I've taken some creative liberties, the stories in this book are all true and happened as described, to the best of my middle-aged memory.

These events could not have happened in another time. The climate that existed between 1979 and 1994 spawned the perfect storm in which rock music flourished and lifelong relationships were formed between artists and their fans. Now, artists burn hot for a few months, then disappear. But in the '80s and '90s, superstars were born and legacies were built that lasted for decades. Artists not only knew how to write songs, play instruments and perform—they had something to say.

During this fifteen-year span, a collaboration was forged between radio stations, record labels, music retailers, and concert promoters. Four different industries united to give artists a platform on which to become superstars. After years of "rock famine," record labels hit pay dirt and stocked record store shelves with quintessential albums from rock's greatest bands. As bands gained a following, concert promoters bellied up to the trough. Outdoor amphitheaters (known as "sheds") sprang up across the country, and concerts routinely sold out. Ticket prices were reasonable, which left fans with a few bucks to buy artist merchandise. Band swag became such big business that many groups earned more money selling T-shirts than performing.

At the heart of this rock renaissance was radio. Popular stations were the megaphone that exposed music and fanned the flames. In radio's glory days, stations had a personality, an attitude. The DJs were your lifeline to exciting, new songs. They were tour guides who got you hooked and brought the music to life. In short, radio was fun, inspiring, and unpredictable.

Now turn that business model on its head and fast-forward to today.

The music landscape has been bulldozed, and the thrill of music discovery has moved to the internet. Before the digital age, music fans had only two options: listen to songs on the radio or buy the album. There were no iPods. There was no YouTube, SiriusXM, or Pandora. So, radio stations were the only launch pad for new bands and wielded tremendous influence. In reality, without radio's support, artists stood little chance of survival.

Clearly, it's a different world now. Record companies have lost their influence. They continue driving through the rearview mirror, hoping that music fans will pay for outdated, expensive CDs. Since the advent of social media, bands can build a loyal following without the support of a record company. Most music fans find the songs that they want online, without paying for them. Once that shift happened, record stores all but disappeared.

As for commercial radio, most rock stations have lost their relevance. Radio's innovative spirit has been surgically removed and replaced by predictable jukeboxes. Stations that once had soul and character have been transformed into indistinguishable blobs of white bread. It's hard to listen now that every second has been sold, sponsored and bartered. In radio's better days, you never knew what was coming next. Now, there's no mystery. You'll hear the same songs today that you heard yesterday.

So, what caused this fundamental change in the radio industry?

In radio's heyday, stations competed for your affection. Battling against other stations got the creative juices flowing and kept us sharp. By the mid-1990s, radio's innovative spirit was snuffed out when the broadcasting industry expe-

rienced a seismic shift. In 1996 the FCC passed the Telecommunications Act. It relaxed the ownership rules that originally allowed a broadcasting company to own one AM station and one FM station in the same city. This new ruling blew the lid off of ownership limits, allowing companies to buy hundreds of radio stations. Hedge funds financed the acquisition of the largest radio stations and strip-mined their resources. This led to a corporate land grab that allowed owners to operate five, six or seven stations in the same city. Companies swallowed up their competitors, and consolidation took hold. The vast majority of stations are now controlled by a few companies who are intent on squeezing the last few dollars out of their stations.

Instead of establishing a long-term vision, accountants focused on quarterly returns. Stations were gutted and starved for resources, with no eye on the future. The thrill of experimentation and collaboration came to a grinding halt as songs became filler sandwiched between commercials. This shoved radio's creative mission to the backseat, if not out of the car.

Meanwhile, consolidation also transformed the concert industry. A few independent promoters still exist. But most have been sucked under the wheels of Live Nation. It's nearly impossible to buy good tickets nowadays without having to overpay an after-market broker. With the exception of the biggest tours, this "bleed the customer" strategy is backfiring.

As for record companies, they're still trying to build walls in the ocean and have chosen the wrong path at every turn. Napster changed the rules and opened the barn doors to file sharing. Rather than trying to harness digital downloads, record companies sued Napster's founder. Apple's iTunes, Spotify and others turned the record-buying model on its head. And now, labels are paying the price. Music fans no

longer needed to spend $12 for an album with one good song. They have a plethora of options.

Record stores are a fading memory. They were once destinations where fans could spend hours pawing through record bins, discovering new music. Now record stores are virtually nonexistent, reduced to novelty shops and a few shelves at Walmart. Technology rendered record stores obsolete and transformed the music listening experience online.

After decades of innovation, radio broadcasters are intent on swallowing their own tail. While radio was once the hub for all music activity, broadcasters have shirked their role as leaders in music discovery. Instead, station owners focus on efficiencies and operate their radio stations like McDonald's franchises. Now, every market has sound-alike, cookie-cutter replicas of KISS, HOT, MAGIC and LITE music formats. Most personalities have been chased out of radio in favor of pre-recorded "voice tracks," often recorded by people who live elsewhere. Gone are live DJs, localism, and the creative spirit. It's now common for an office of five radio stations to be totally canned. The only movement is the flashing lights on the automation system. Literally, not a single, live person is in the building. There is nobody there to take your requests, celebrate the music, and plot to undermine the competition. Today, there's a good chance that your favorite radio station is a soulless hard drive.

Gone are the days of gut instinct. Today, song research dictates the music you hear on the radio. Every tune has been meticulously tested, analyzed, homogenized and had its demographic appeal scientifically coded before getting on the air. Don't bother calling the station's request line. It's been scrapped as an "unnecessary expense." Now, listeners are herded into focus groups and observed through two-way glass. Song playlists are computer-generated and printed out on music logs days in advance. Radio program-

mers are now told by corporate bosses what to play. They meekly follow a safe, prescribed path without ever breaking new ground...or taking the risk of getting fired.

There are two divided camps about the future of radio.

The first likes the future just the way it is and believes that radio will survive against a tidal wave of challengers.

The second camp believes that if music radio were a movie, they'd be rolling the credits.

Yes, it was fun while it lasted, but sadly, I think this movie is almost over.

BP

RANDOM SHOTS

*Tommy Shaw from Styx shows off his
Coleco video game player*

Alice Cooper without his boa snake or makeup

Beau with Joe Walsh, our morning DJ and Rick "the bass player" Rosas

Fishing with Bad Company's Paul Rodgers

259

Quiet Riot's Kevin DuBrow and Carlos Cavazo